TO CROSS A RIVER

JIMMY SWAGGART

WITH ROBERT PAUL LAMB

LOGOS INTERNATIONAL
PLAINFIELD, NEW JERSEY

Second Edition August 1, 1977

TO CROSS A RIVER
Copyright © 1977 by Logos International
All rights reserved
Printed in the United States of America
International Standard Book Number: 0-88270-221-1
Library of Congress Catalog Card Number: 77-73152
Published by Logos International
Plainfield, New Jersey 07061

DEDICATION

From the very beginning, God gave me a very special woman to be my helpmate. The things which have been accomplished in my ministry would have never been done without her help. No man could ask for more and no man could be more thankful. This story is lovingly dedicated to her — Frances Anderson Swaggart.

Commit thy way unto the Lord,
trust also in him,
and he shall bring it to pass.
Psalm 37:5

Contents

PREFACE

When people, even friends, discovered I was writing the story of a Christian personality with the public visibility of Jimmy Swaggart, they often asked: "Is he for real? Are there skeletons in the closet?"

In a day when there are many voices in the land, when it's difficult to distinguish between the tares and the wheat, those questions are not surprising ones—even when asked about Christian ministers.

Happily, in Jimmy's case, I can honestly say he's genuine, and there are no skeletons in any Swaggart closet. Everything is open and aboveboard.

Once, in a television interview, Jimmy described himself as an "old-fashioned, Holy-Ghost-filled, shouting, weeping, soul-winning, gospel-preaching preacher. I wouldn't be anything else."

That's essentially the person I found in the writing of this book. Whether he was recounting his boyhood days in the quiet of his home, or eating hamburgers (his favorite meal) over the noisy tables of Wesley's in Baton Rouge, or preaching and singing to thousands in a packed auditorium in Little Rock, I found Jimmy the same. Warm. Friendly. Sincere. And totally dedicated to serving the Lord Jesus Christ.

"I could do this twenty-four hours a day," Jimmy said in that recent television interview. "I'm the kind who gets mad at going to sleep at night. Living for Jesus Christ is not some dragged out, dreary, tiptoing through the tulips thing. It's still the greatest thing going today."

Yeah, it is, Jimmy.

Robert Paul Lamb
Charlotte, North Carolina

FOREWORD

There is something profoundly true in this book. You'll have to dig for it as you read, because I'm not sure that even Jimmy Swaggart realizes the impact of the spiritual principles he has chosen to follow. Very few of God's men do. That's the reason they need someone else to tell their story for them. In this case it was my good friend, Robert Paul Lamb, who did the hard work of ferreting out, not only the facts, but the principles which operate in Jimmy's life to make him a success.

This is more than the story of a backwoods Pentecostal preacher from the bayous of Louisiana who "made it big." I have no excitement about that kind of book. If I spend money for a book, and take time to read it, I want something which will help me, which will show me a better way.

But the way we find as we read Jimmy's book, while it is infinitely better, is not easy. Jimmy could have gone the "way of the world"—as some of his equally famous kinsmen did. Instead, he chose the narrow road, the road walked by his father and mother—choosing to spend the rest of his days in the swamps and bogs of Louisiana if God so desired.

For a time it looked like he was doomed to that

same ministerial mediocrity which is the fate of so many struggling preachers. Then, because of the principles he chose to follow, he suddenly rounded a curve in the road and stepped into a worldwide ministry.

Yet the pitfalls of walking in success, he found, were even greater than those along the road leading to it. Only by living by those same principles which had become his way of life could he keep that which God had given him.

That's the reason I am excited about this book. It is more than the typical success story. It is the story of a man—and his family—who discovered that while the way of God is not easy, it is glorious. And in the end, it pays far more than all the world can offer.

Jamie Buckingham

1
TO CROSS
A RIVER

Once to every man and nation comes the moment to decide, in the strife of Truth with Falsehood, for the good or evil side.

–James Russell Lowell
The Present Crisis

The sleek, black Cadillac skidded in the gravel as it rounded the little Assembly of God church and pulled to a crunching stop. It was late spring of 1958 and hardly anybody—at least in Pentecostal circles—drove Cadillacs. But my Uncle Elmo wasn't just anybody. He was my cousin Jerry Lee Lewis's dad. And everybody knew that Jerry Lee and Elvis Presley were the two biggest names in rock-and-roll music. Tall and lanky, Uncle Elmo was always in a hurry. He never

1

seemed to stay in one place long enough to make friends, yet he was the kind who had never met a stranger.

Leaving the engine idling and the door open, he jumped out of the car and ran toward me. "Man," he said, grabbing my arms, "do I have news for you!"

For a piano-playing Pentecostal preacher in the backwoods of Louisiana, struggling to support a wife and three-year-old son, any news from a Cadillac-driving uncle had to be good. Recently the offerings hadn't even been enough to pay for gas to drive to church, much less put food on the table. Day-to-day living had become an unbelievable struggle.

"I've just left Memphis," Uncle Elmo grinned, "and Sam Phillips has sent for you."

Sam Phillips was about the most famous record producer in the world in the late 1950s. He was the man who had discovered Elvis Presley, Johnny Cash, Charlie Rich and my cousin, Jerry Lee.

Jerry Lee and I had been raised together. Even though we were first cousins, we were actually as close as brothers. At times it seemed as if we were twins. But things had changed. Jerry Lee was now big time. He was making more than twenty thousand dollars a week and the papers called him "the wild man of rock-and-roll." I was struggling along on thirty dollars a week—sometimes even less—as a small time, wrong-side-of-the-tracks

Pentecostal preacher.

Uncle Elmo was still rattling on. ". . . and you play the piano like Jerry Lee and you sing. In fact, some folks can't tell your piano styles apart. Sam already knows you're good. Real good. He told me to have you in Memphis first thing Monday morning and the contracts would be ready. So I've come to get you."

"Now hold on, Uncle Elmo," I said, backing off. "I can't do that. You know I don't play that stuff. I'm a preacher."

"Oh," he laughed, "I forgot to tell you. Sam wants to start a gospel line for Sun Records. RCA has one. Columbia has one. Now Sun is going to start one. You'll be their first gospel artist."

My imagination ran wild. Records meant money, big money. Now we could have a new car and a house of our own. Frances could buy a pretty dress. Maybe we could even save some money for Donnie to go to college. All those things I had dreamed of but never had. All mine—with one stroke of the pen.

I wanted so badly to say, "I'm ready! Let's leave right now." But the words just wouldn't come out. Something—someone—seemed to wire my jaws together. And inside, I felt this compelling urgency to say "no." I knew it was the Lord but I couldn't believe He'd tell me to refuse this offer.

"No, you can't go," the words rang in my ears. "This is something you can't do." The words were

3

so forceful I had to put my hands on one of the food-laden tables to steady myself. I looked around at the people in the churchyard. It was Sunday afternoon of an all-day meeting with dinner on the grounds. They were all poor but honest folks. Could I really turn my back on them for money?

Uncle Elmo looked at me strangely as the expression on my face changed. "What's the matter?" he asked.

"Well," I answered haltingly, "I can't go."

"Did I hear you right?"

"I'm sorry," I said, and turned my head away. My eyes were burning with tears. The crowd of folks all around were laughing and talking, but it was as though I had stepped into an aura of holy silence. It was as though time had stopped. Even the sparrows in the nearby willow trees had stopped their twittering.

Uncle Elmo ran his hand impulsively through his straight, black hair. "Jimmy, don't you realize what this could mean? This is the man who started Elvis Presley, Johnny Cash and Charlie Rich. I'll bet there are ten thousand people who'd give their right arms for ten minutes with Sam Phillips. And he's sent for you! I've got it all set up, and now you're telling me you can't go."

"I'm sorry," I answered again as my embarrassment grew.

He scratched his head. "But it's gospel music,"

4

he said. "You couldn't object to that."

"No, it's not that," I said. "It's something else."

"Look at that old car," he suggested, pointing to my rusted old hulk. "Don't you know it's all to pieces? And your clothes. I've seen you in that same suit a dozen times."

He was right. My battered, blue Plymouth was literally falling apart. Frances had only four cotton dresses. Donnie had so few clothes they could have been carried in a sack. All I had was a twenty dollar Stein suit and a single pair of shoes. We couldn't afford our own home, and had to stay in church basements, pastors' homes and small hotels. Some nights we went to bed hungry. Yet I knew the answer was still no. I couldn't go to Memphis.

"Uncle Elmo, I know you're trying to help me," I said trying to make amends for my refusal, "and I love you and appreciate you for it."

"How much money are you making here?" he asked.

"About thirty dollars a week."

"In thirty days you'll be able to buy a new Cadillac—and pay cash! I personally guarantee it. You play and sing better than many of the top entertainers today. You've got talent. Ability. Looks. Everything you need to become famous. You'll be rich."

"I can't do it."

We stood long moments, looking at one

5

another. "You mean you'd turn down all that for" and he waved his arm toward the crowd of church folk "for this?"

I nodded.

He shook his head and started back toward his car. Then he returned, grabbed my hand in both of his, and squeezed it tightly. "I think I understand." And he was gone.

As the Cadillac turned out of sight, an overwhelming temptation came over me to run after him and hail him down. I felt foolish and terribly alone. My uncle had gone out on a limb to help me and I had embarrassed him. How many times had he filled my gas tank? Put groceries on my table? Now he was trying to do even more, and I had turned him down. Had I done right? Was it God who had wired my jaws shut, or Satan? Right now the Lord seemed to be a million miles away.

Normally I enjoyed these church dinners on the grounds. Sometimes it was the only chance to eat decently. But my appetite had disappeared.

I left the people still eating and talking over the dinner tables. Many of them had been impressed with Uncle Elmo's Cadillac and they talked of Jerry Lee's fame and fortune. I walked inside the little white frame building where I had been preaching a week-long revival. Inside I found one of the smelly Sunday school rooms where I wouldn't be interrupted, and leaned against a wall.

"Lord, why?" I asked as tears ran down my face. "I've told you I'd serve you. You know I'll preach your gospel if I've got to hitchhike to do it. I wanted to say yes so badly, but you wouldn't let me. Why?"

Thoughts of my family's pressing needs began flooding through my mind. It appeared as if I had passed up an excellent opportunity to help my family. For some reason, I had made a decision that was beyond me. In my mind I could see new cars, fine suits, clothes for my family. Things we desperately needed.

There was no earthquake, no thunder and lightning, no roaring voice. But inside the Lord began to speak. "Son, I'm going to tell you two things about this. First, I have better plans for you. If you accepted this offer, I could never use you as I desire. Second, trust me. Even though it doesn't look good now, I promise that you won't be disappointed."

Trust me.

The words stood out strongly. "I can't see anything but living in poverty and preaching in some backwoods church, Lord, but I'll do it. I'll trust you."

As I walked out of that Sunday school room, I still felt that overwhelming desire to run find Uncle Elmo. But I didn't. I knew I had leaped a giant hurdle. I had crossed an unfordable river.

The immediate future hadn't changed. It still looked bleak and gloomy. I didn't know where the next dollar or revival meeting was coming from, but I was determined to trust God.

In my heart I knew I had made the right choice.

2
FERRIDAY, LOUISIANA

Some eighty miles south of Monroe and eighty-five miles northwest of Baton Rouge, Louisiana's capital city, is Ferriday, located at the northern part of Concordia Parish. It was my home, for as long as I could remember and then some. Bordered by the Mississippi River on the East and the Tensas, Black, and Red Rivers on the West, Concordia Parish is part of one of the richest agricultural regions in Louisiana.

Prior to the fall of 1903, Ferriday was just a

cotton field, part of the Helena Plantation. Then the Texas & Pacific and Iron Mountain railways chose that particular cotton field as a terminal and site for their railroad shops. Three years later Ferriday—named after an early owner of the plantation—was incorporated.

Jobs were scarce during the Great Depression, but a variety of saw mills and cotton warehouses combined to keep many folks employed. Others turned to the fertile delta soil for a living through farming, or to the Mississippi River and its meandering tributaries for trapping and fishing.

It was the fishing and trapping that brought my father, Willie Leon Swaggart, and my grandfather, Willie Harry Swaggart, whom we called Pa, to Ferriday. Vast numbers of families were migrating throughout the country in search of work during this time. Many people, particularly in the South, were loading all of their possessions on trucks and heading off to what they hoped would be better lives. One of those families was the Swaggarts, who moved into a small, frame house on Third Avenue.

Still in his middle teens, dad was an excellent musician and in great demand as a fiddle player. His income was pretty evenly divided between working in the fields during the day and playing at the dances throughout Concordia Parish at night. The old-fashioned hoedowns and square dances were one of the few ways the people could work off the tensions of the depression.

During one of these dances, which sometimes erupted into first-class brawls, daddy met Minnie Bell Herron. Before moving to Ferriday in the early 1930s, the Herron family had been poor sharecroppers in several Louisiana parishes, moving often, always on the brink of starvation.

Daddy was nineteen, and mama seventeen, when they married. They, too, were looking for some way out of the trap of poverty. But their living conditions hardly improved after they married. In fact, during the early months of 1935, practically every member of the family—plus an assortment of other relatives—went into bootlegging whiskey just to make enough money to survive.

One day the entire clan was out in the backwoods near Turtle Lake, working on the illegal whiskey when they were raided by federal revenue agents. The agents loaded their pickup truck with all my arrested relatives and were driving down the dirt road to the main highway when they met mama walking toward them. My parents had been married about a year and mama was already pregnant with me.

The pickup stopped briefly. "Who is she?" an agent seated in the back of the truck asked daddy.

"That's my wife," my father answered, feeling guilty that his pregnant wife had to see him under arrest.

The agent paused, then shrugged. He knew what poverty was like, too. "Well, you get her out of here," he said to daddy. "And if I see you around here a minute longer, you're going to jail."

Daddy grabbed mama and took off down the road but all the other relatives, including five of my uncles, wound up behind bars.

Two months later I was born—March 15, 1935, at the home of my uncle, Lee Calhoun, who lived a few miles outside of Ferriday off the Jonesville highway. I was named Jimmy Lee after him.

Although an uneducated and rough man, Uncle Lee was wealthy by Louisiana standards and even though he had actually been the brains behind the bootlegging business, he was well-respected in the community. He never seemed to have the problems all my other relatives had. Shortly after I was born he had been caught with a truckload of cattle and arrested for cattle rustling. Miraculously, Uncle Lee was able to prove in court, by producing a number of eye witnesses—a few of whom owed him money—that he was actually hauling horses, not cows.

Uncle Lee seemed to arouse deep feelings of love or hate with everyone he did business with. Perhaps it was because of his forceful personality and the loud profanity he constantly used. He was the kind of man whose loud, booming voice was heard long before you ever saw him. His house was constantly full of people looking for money, politicians asking for favors, and preachers hoping for some kind of contribution.

The Assemblies of God, founded twenty-two years earlier in 1914, were part of a vast evangelical movement that swept most of the South and Midwest during the roaring twenties and depression thirties.

It was not unusual for missionaries of the church to bring the message of Pentecost into various areas of the country. During 1936, two women from Laurel, Mississippi—Mother Sumrall and her young daughter, Leona—came to Ferriday and put seats and benches out in the open on a vacant lot.

The Sumralls didn't have a car so they walked up and down the streets knocking on doors and inviting people to what would ultimately become an Assembly of God church.

One day while Uncle Lee was driving through Ferriday, he turned onto Texas Street and caught a glimpse of the two Sumrall women pulling weeds with their bare hands on the vacant lot. He stopped his truck and asked what they were doing.

"We're going to build a church here," Mother Sumrall announced pleasantly, standing up and wiping sweat from her face.

"And who's financing this project?" Uncle Lee asked, always looking for a lucrative business deal.

"God is!" she answered. "The Lord sent us here and we're just doing this in obedience."

"God?" Uncle Lee repeated with a quizzical look on his face. "You mean God actually spoke to you?"

"That's right!" Mother Sumrall answered with a smile. "He sure did."

Uncle Lee walked back to his truck. He'd never heard of such talk. His whole life had been wrapped up in money. How could these two women say that God spoke to them?

The Sumralls ultimately got the lot cleared and began services under a tent. People throughout the parish began filtering into the services. Daddy heard the stirring music at the services one night and later decided to join in and play his fiddle. Soon mama, an accomplished rhythm guitar player and singer, came along.

It was daddy's first time in a church service. Mama had been to three funerals as a child, but neither of them knew anything about God. In fact, they didn't own a Bible. Yet, there was something about the music—

Night after night as they sat through the services, the Spirit of the Lord dealt with them. Daddy was deeply troubled about accepting Jesus as his Saviour. He felt he'd have to give up some of

14

his plans for making money if he surrendered his life to Christ. And things were just about to open up in the trapping and fur business.

Daddy couldn't take the conflict and decided to run. Somehow he felt this deep conviction would be gone if they moved eight hundred miles away to Texas.

Daddy sold his small plot of land outside of Ferriday, along with our small, three-room house. He loaded our few possessions on the Ford pickup and left for Rio Hondo, Texas, in the heart of the fertile Rio Grande valley.

Being a very grown-up four-year-old, I got to stand on the transmission hump and peer out the windshield as I pretended to navigate the truck. Mama was holding little Donnie, who was only a few weeks old, in her lap. She was singing a song she had learned at the tent meeting, "I Know the Lord Will Make a Way for Me."

It had been freezing cold when we left Ferriday but it was warm enough to go barefooted in Texas. Bright sunshine filled each day and the scent of citrus blossoms was constantly in the air.

But once in Texas, all of daddy's plans for making money backfired. He was like a Jonah on the ship, and everyone else began to suffer, too. Mama and the new baby came down with pneumonia. Both were admitted to a hospital. "There's no problem, Mr. Swaggart," a doctor told my father. "You don't have anything to worry

15

about. I've never lost a patient with pneumonia."

The druggist gave him the same reassurance. "You don't have anything to worry about," he said. "This doctor is one of the best. I know him."

But daddy was troubled. He tried to pray, but there was no answer. Only a deep fear that little Donnie was going to die.

Four days later daddy woke up with a fever and cough—pneumonia. There was a knock at the door of our room in the old tourist court.

"Who is it?" Daddy asked weakly.

"Frank," came the reply beyond the door.

Lying in the bed beside my father, I recognized the voice. It was Uncle Frank. He was a smiling, happy man but I noticed when he opened the door he wasn't smiling or happy. I could see him framed in the early morning light with his head bowed, shoulders humped. I pulled the covers up around my face as the cold air rushed into the room.

Daddy raised up beside me on one elbow, coughing. "Frank, what is it?"

Uncle Frank didn't answer.

Daddy started weeping. I didn't understand what was happening but I knew it was bad. Daddy was sobbing so hard the whole bed was shaking.

"Donnie's dead, isn't he?" daddy finally choked out.

Uncle Frank started crying, too. "Yes, he is."

16

Two days later, with mama still in the hospital, some men came to help daddy get dressed and into the truck. A small handful of people were standing quietly as we drove to the gravesite. Uncle Frank and another man helped daddy from the truck and I walked alongside him to the grave.

The tiny casket was opened and tears fell from daddy's eyes as he looked at the baby. "I know my baby would be alive if I had lived for God," he whispered. "It's all my fault."

Donnie's death weighed heavily on my father. He vowed if he could just get back to Ferriday he would give his life to God. But once back home, he didn't. Instead, he and mama began fighting continuously. Both were high-tempered people. They were constantly screaming at each other. Afterwards I'd hear mama alone in her room crying.

It had been like that ever since they married, but now it was worse. One time, in the heat of an argument over whether mama would cook black-eyed peas for daddy, she tossed the whole pan full of peas into the front yard. There was no other food in the house and Uncle Elmo and Aunt Mamie, Jerry Lee's parents, picked up most of the peas. The black-eyed peas and cornbread had a peculiar taste that night. No one spoke at the table.

By the summer of 1941, the Assembly of God church had been built in Ferriday. Somehow, God had touched Uncle Lee's heart (and billfold) through the efforts of the two Sumrall women. He had donated all of the money to build the little white frame church. Once the structure was up, the Sumralls moved on to other pioneer works and Tom Holcomb came as the pastor.

The church was financially unable to support Brother Holcomb. For a while he worked in Texas during the week, and drove back to Ferriday to preach on the weekend. Then his young son, like little Donnie, died suddenly with pneumonia.

During the months following the Holcomb child's death, mama and daddy watched them carefully. They saw something different in the Holcombs. There was no bitterness toward God, no guilt. Mama and daddy recognized the Holcombs had something special. It left a mark on their lives.

Still daddy wasn't ready to surrender.

After the war broke out in December of 1941, daddy and mama moved to Temple, Texas, to work temporarily in a defense plant. Once again, we had a new baby going with us, my sister, Jeanette. I attended school briefly in Texas, but it was a madhouse. Thousands of people had moved to Temple because of the high wages being paid defense workers. The schools were unprepared to

18

handle such a load. For several weeks there was a shortage of desks and I, along with many others, had to sit on the floor.

It wasn't long before my parents, desperately homesick for Ferriday, returned to Louisiana. This time they moved into a larger house on Tyler Road.

Blossoms were already on the trees and spring was in the air when we finally settled. I was seven years old and glad to be back among family and friends.

Shortly after we settled back in Ferriday for what daddy said was "keeps," Vincent Roccaforte, a young evangelist, came to town. Years before his mother had been dramatically healed of cancer at a meeting conducted by Raymond T. Richey. The healing transformed the entire Roccaforte family, and ultimately led young Vincent into the ministry.

During the revival, as he shared the story, something happened in daddy's life. This was the kind of God they had been waiting to know, a God of miracles. If He could heal a woman dying of cancer, and turn a Catholic boy into a Pentecostal evangelist, maybe He could touch their lives, too. That night, with tears on his face, daddy walked down the aisle and surrendered his life to Christ. Following him, only a few steps behind was mama. Behind her were daddy's parents.

Everything changed. Mama and daddy no

longer fought. Our home was happy and peaceful. I couldn't have been happier.

We had no electricity at the time and there were no street lights to help find our way to church over on Texas Street. Every time we got ready for church it seemed like it would rain. But mama and daddy were serious about their relationship with God. We went to church regardless of darkness or water. Often daddy and I pulled off our shoes and rolled up our trousers to the knees to avoid the water while mama put her stockings in her hands. Sometimes we all waded through the drenching rain. Occasionally it would be so dark, we'd have to wait for the lightning to flash so we could see the way around the deep mud holes. But it was fun. Life had become fun.

I enjoyed Sunday school particularly. I always liked reading, and when the teacher read I sat quietly just picturing all the scenes being played out before my eyes. David and Goliath was my favorite story. Many times I sat pretending it was me hitting the giant with the rock.

Mama had been a Christian for over a year when she began talking to me about getting saved. Although I was just eight years old, I knew Jesus from the Bible lessons at church and Sunday school. I knew He was the Son of God. I also knew, like daddy, that He would require something of me if I called Him Lord.

I loved going to the movies at the Arcade

Theatre on Fourth Avenue. Mama had been a frequent moviegoer, too, but once she became a Christian she decided to quit going. But it had been a real battle.

"You really shouldn't go," were her last words to me that Saturday as I left the house for the walk uptown. My cousins, Jerry Lee Lewis and Mickey Gilley, normally went with me. But this Saturday I was alone.

Saturday afternoons were fairly routine. I'd walk uptown to see one of my favorite cowboy stars, Johnny Mack Brown, Gene Autry or Hopalong Cassidy. Sometimes there'd be a special serial showing. The rest of the afternoon was spent among boys my age acting out some of the cowboy roles we'd seen on the silver screen.

That day, there was a line of kids standing and waiting for the three o'clock movie. I patiently waited until I got to the front of the line, then laid my quarter down. Mrs. Green, the gray-haired ticket seller, was busy trying to fix one of the winding rolls of tickets.

As I stood waiting, an entreating voice suddenly spoke to me. "Do not go in this place. Give your heart to me. I have chosen you a vessel to be used in my service."

The voice was so firm, yet loving, I was almost hypnotized by it. I didn't know what to do. I looked around to see if somebody was talking to me. Something inside seemed to say it was God

21

speaking to me. I began to cry.

Mrs. Green was still laboring over the tickets and actually hadn't even noticed me. "This is my imagination," I thought. "I want to see this movie."

But the voice spoke again. "Do not go in this place. Give your heart to me. I have chosen you a vessel to be used in my service." The words were so strong chill bumps broke out on my arm. My hair tingled. Somehow the words had so much power, I couldn't resist them. I had to yield.

"I will, I'll do what you said," I responded to the voice which I knew belonged to the Lord. "I'll accept you."

Mrs. Green had finally finished her task and was now glaring at me over her rimless glasses. "Jimmy, do you want to go?" she asked. "If not, there are others behind you."

I stepped aside and began skipping down the street. "I've got a home in glory land that outshines the sun, I've got a home in glory land that outshines the sun," I sang. I felt twenty pounds lighter. I had never felt so good. I had decided to follow Jesus. It didn't even bother me I had missed the Saturday afternoon Johnny Mack Brown movie. To celebrate, I stopped off at Vogt's Drug Store on the corner and got a double scoop ice cream cone.

When I arrived home that afternoon, mama was ironing. "Why are you back home so early?"

she questioned while pushing a steaming iron over a green print dress.

"I didn't go to the movie," I said sitting down at the kitchen table to finish my ice cream.

"Why?" she asked.

"I gave my heart to the Lord and I'm not going any more."

The room was quiet for a few moments. When I looked up, tears were filling mama's eyes. "Jimmy, I'm so thrilled," she said softly. "This makes me so happy. I couldn't be more pleased."

Everything seemed different after that day in front of the Arcade Theatre. I felt better inside. Almost like taking a bath continuously, I felt good and clean. A song seemed to bubble in my heart.

3
"NANNIE'S GONE CRAZY OVER RELIGION!"

During the war years of the early 1940s, Pa Swaggart served as chief of police in Ferriday. Before he had taken the job, you could hardly walk down the street without getting a beer bottle laid against your head. The mayor, in fact, had hired several police chiefs before, but the drunks, bullies and "case hards" had run them off.

Although Fort Polk was located in Alexandria, fifty miles away, Ferriday with its bars became a popular hangout for the soldiers. Only the heaviest drinkers got this far, and they were mean and tough. But Pa cleaned up the town. He was a thick, powerful man who often noted that "nobody ever whipped him."

Yet as chief of police, he never pulled his pistol in ten years on the job. He didn't have to. People said there was something about the way he turned those steel-gray eyes on a man. Folks knew that he was a man who meant business.

I stayed with my grandparents about as much as I did with my own mother and father. Pa seemed to love it, even when I was constantly unpinning his badge and trying on his police cap. My grandmother, Ada, was the same way. I could never pronounce "Grannie" properly, so I shortened it to "Nannie" and pretty soon everybody else called her that too.

Before she had become a Christian, Nannie was like the rest of the Swaggarts. She enjoyed drinking, smoking and even a little gambling. But at the age of forty-five, a dramatic change had occurred in her life. Shortly afterward she went to a Church of God camp meeting being held near Snake Ridge. When she returned to Ferriday, she was totally different. She had received the Baptism in the Holy Spirit and was speaking in tongues. Not only that but she was delightfully happy, bubbly. And the cigarette habit, which she hadn't been able to shake despite her conversion, was gone.

Nannie was preaching to everybody in earshot. "You've got to get it. You've got to have it. You really don't know the Lord like you should until you receive it."

My parents, even though they belonged to the little twenty-five-member Assembly of God church, had never heard of the Baptism in the Holy Spirit. Nannie's strange doctrine infuriated them. In fact, they openly rejected her and called her a fanatic. As the situation pressed on, mama finally went to the church's new pastor, Henry Culbreth.

"Brother Culbreth," she said seriously, "am I saved?"

"Yes, you are," he replied.

"Do I have to have this experience with the Holy Spirit and speak in tongues to be saved?" she questioned.

"No, you don't."

"Well, in that case," mama replied, "I don't want anything to do with it. It's too fanatical for me."

Even though mama and daddy were fighting Nannie's experience, I was thrilled about it. Every opportunity I had, I went to her house and asked her to explain the story all over again.

"Jimmy," she'd say, "you know when I went to that camp meeting I was so hungry for the Lord. Those services lasted almost twenty-four hours a day. When one preacher finished, we'd sing and then another would start. The services never seemed to end.

"But one day I was standing outside the little tabernacle near a grove of trees praying with my brother John and his wife. The presence of God became so real. Suddenly it seemed as if I had been struck by a bolt of lightning. Lying flat on my back, I raised my hands to praise the Lord. No English came out. Only unknown tongues."

Everytime Nannie told that story the power of God would hit her again, and she would begin to speak in tongues. Sitting on the floor near her chair, the power of the Lord would run all over me, too. Chill bumps would break out on my arms. The roots of my hair tingled. I would begin crying. The only thing that rivaled the experience in my life was that day I stood in front of the Arcade Theatre, and said to God, "I will."

School was out and in the early summer of 1943 I spent hours at Nannie's house on Mississippi Avenue, listening to her story. Every time I asked her to tell it again she would laugh and say, "Let me fix a cup of hot tea first and then I'll tell you."

Then she would sit down in that same easy chair and begin telling me the story again. I sat cross-legged on the floor and braced myself for the point when the power would hit her. It would always happen all over again, like a ball of fire rolling down on her, and hitting me, too.

I would come back that afternoon with the same request. "Nannie, tell me how God filled you with the Holy Ghost." Day after day, this went on. She never tired of telling the story to me.

Mama and daddy were still opposed to Nannie's preaching. One morning I jumped out of bed, hit a lick at my hair and was tearing off the front porch when daddy caught me by the neck of my shirt.

"Where you going, boy?" he demanded sternly.

I had heard him and mama say Nannie had gone crazy over religion and I knew I was treading on thin ice. "I'm just going out," I tried to alibi.

"No, you're not," he said. "You're going to my mama's."

I tried to think of something to say.

"She's filling your head full of junk," he said.

"Well—"

"Nannie's gone crazy over religion," he said forcefully. "If you go back again, I'm going to tear you up!"

I hung around the porch until daddy went back into the house. Then I beat a quick retreat to Nannie's. "Tell me again," I said as soon as I got there. Daddy never found out.

That summer, J.M. Cason, an evangelist, came to the little church on Texas Street to hold revival services. It was his first revival, he explained, and he had only three sermons. "When I finish those, I'll have to start over," he said honestly.

In spite of his inexperience as a preacher, the people packed the church building to hear him.

29

He was a highly emotional man who cried and preached at the same time. Eventually, he would just stop preaching and tell the people to give their lives to God. The crowds jammed the altar.

One night Brother Cason was so excited all he could do was shout. Over and over he hollered, "Praise the Lord! Praise the Lord! Praise the Lord!"

Mama and daddy were offended by Brother Cason's conduct. Daddy, who had finally begun to make money, was also making an attempt at community dignity. He and mama complained about Brother Cason's emotional explosions to the pastor and asked him to close down the meeting immediately.

Pastor Culbreth was a wise man. "God will take care of it," he said smiling. "In fact, we're going to start a morning prayer meeting to give the revival more support."

Mama and daddy were furious. Yet for some reason they continued going to the revival, as well as the morning prayer meeting. They complained all the time, yet used the excuse, "It's our church and no weird preacher is going to drive us away." It was just the opening God needed to invade their lives. The more they listened to Brother Cason the more they recognized he wasn't a wild-eyed fanatic. He was just a normal Christian, what every believer in Jesus should be. Like me, they were infected with a hunger for more.

Several mornings later, while Brother Cason was playing his accordion and leading the song, "By and By When the Morning Comes," things began to happen in the service. It was like the original Pentecost as "the Holy Ghost fell on all them which heard the word."

Aunt Mamie, Jerry Lee's mother, had just returned to her seat after a trip to the altar, when the power of God fell on the congregation. She leaped up and started running back down the aisle to the altar. Halfway down the aisle she fell to the floor. When she came up she was speaking in tongues.

Irene Gilley, Nannie's sister, was kneeling in the corner beside the altar. As the Spirit fell, she, too, began to speak in tongues.

Weeks before mama had complained, "This shouting, yelling and hollering is ridiculous. I'll never do it."

But that morning she did all the things she boasted she would never do. She ran around the building, hollering, dancing in the Spirit, and before she got back to her seat—speaking in tongues.

I hadn't gone to the meeting that morning. In fact, I was playing several blocks away from the church with Jerry Lee and the two Stone brothers, Mack and Huey P. When we heard someone shouting at the top of his lungs, we all stopped and listened.

31

"What's that?" Mack asked.

A dread swept over my heart. I knew it was my mother and I was embarrassed for her as well as myself. I knew she and daddy were at church but I couldn't imagine what was happening.

The scream came again. "It's coming from that church," Mack said loudly.

"No," I responded. "It's probably just a wreck."

"Well, let's go see." Everybody but me quickly agreed.

"No," I persisted. "They'll probably have it dragged off by the time we get over there. You know how fast the wrecker is at the Texaco station."

I didn't know what had happened but I knew that voice belonged to my mother. She had yelled at me so often I had no problem recognizing it. I just couldn't understand the situation. Mama never did things like that in church.

The other kids raced toward the church. I turned and made a hurried dash for the house. When I got there, Papa Herron was waiting for mama. He had a routine every morning of visiting each of his children and having a cup of coffee with them. His first stop was at mama's, but she had disrupted his routine by staying late at church. He was clearly furious.

I was standing on the screen porch talking with him when daddy and mama drove up. As they got out of the truck, they were both laughing, and mama appeared to be speaking in a strange language.

Papa Herron, still ruffled, started to say, "Where in the—?"

But mama grabbed him and started dancing around the room, still speaking in tongues. Suddenly the power of God descended on him too. Grabbing her shoulders with both hands, tears running down his face, he cried, "Sister, I don't know what they did to you, but it must be wonderful."

That same summer, not only was daddy filled with the Holy Spirit, but so was I. I had wanted to be baptized with the Holy Spirit exactly like Nannie had been, but it didn't happen that way.

At our church, we usually had two altar calls, one for people who wanted to surrender to Christ, another for folks who wanted to receive the Holy Spirit. I went forward almost every Sunday, seeking to be filled with the Holy Spirit. Nothing happened. I was growing desperate.

Then, just before school began, a colorful woman preacher named Thelma Wiggins from Houston, came to lead services in Ferriday. I spent a great deal of time going to the altar. The last night of the services something finally released within me. Kneeling at the altar, praying as usual, I became aware of what seemed to be a brilliant shaft of light descending from heaven and focusing on me. Moments later I was speaking in tongues.

For days afterwards, I spoke very little English. In fact, one day mama sent me to the post office to get a three cent stamp. I placed a nickel down on the counter but instead of telling the clerk I wanted a stamp I began speaking in tongues.

"Son, I can't understand the language you're speaking," the tense little man behind the counter said.

I had been praying about half the day in tongues and didn't think anything about it, but it sure frightened the postal clerk.

I tried again to tell him I wanted a stamp, but it came out in tongues. By this time, I was scared, too. I scooped up the nickel and headed out the front door.

Between my eighth and ninth birthdays, I would frequently go out to a small covering of trees behind our house to pray. I had made an altar from an old log and together with another cousin, Sullivan Herron, I spent hours praying. Ultimately I rubbed the bark completely off the log and wore down the grass around it.

That year Cecil Janway, a boyish-looking preacher, came to our church. Brother Janway was also an accomplished piano player. Night after night, I sat watching as he skillfully played the church's battered upright piano. He brought life from the instrument, life which flowed throughout the church building. I sat close by the piano, fascinated, watching his fingers on the keyboard and listening as he sang. One night while Brother Janway was preaching I started praying, asking God for a miracle.

"Lord," I said, "I want you to give me the gift of playing the piano." I prayed the entire time Brother Janway was preaching. Sometimes I'd get too loud and daddy would reach over and punch me. Then I'd go back to praying under my breath.

I didn't know anything about the world beyond Ferriday, Louisiana, but I made the Lord a solemn promise. "If you give me this talent, I will never use it in the world."

A night club was the most worldly thing I knew about, so I added that to the promise, trying to make it as specific as possible. "I will never play in a night club and I will always use the talent for your glory." Then I added the clincher. "If I ever go back on this promise, you can paralyze my fingers!"

That same night, after Brother Janway had moved away from the platform at the close of the service, I walked over to the piano. I had never tried to play before but I sat down and began making chords. I didn't know what I was doing, but it sounded right.

"Have you been going to Aunt Stella's?" daddy asked when we got back home from church.

"No, sir," I answered trying to explain what I was doing at the church's piano.

"Have you been to Sister Culbreth's house?"

"No, sir."

"Well then, where did you learn those chords?"

"That's what I've been trying to tell you," I explained. "I prayed while Brother Janway was preaching and asked the Lord to give me the talent." I knew it was a beginning which would develop.

My cousin Jerry Lee Lewis was also playing the piano, but I'm not sure if he got his gift the same way I got mine. However, as double first cousins living near one another, we were inseparable. That means we spent a lot of time arguing and fighting.

Although only six months younger, Jerry Lee was one year behind me in school. The last day of school when I passed to the fifth grade, I walked out onto the school grounds on Virginia Avenue and saw him crying.

"What's the matter?" I asked. "Did you get into a fight?" He was constantly in schoolyard fights and as his cousin I frequently had to defend his honor. Word had gotten around that if you picked a fight with Jerry Lee you would have to whip me, too.

"No," he answered unhappily. "I failed."

Jerry Lee handed me his report card. He had

twenty-seven F's.

"Let's go see the teacher," I said, ushering him back toward the schoolhouse. "I know her. She taught me in the third grade."

Mrs. West, the matronly teacher who had failed Jerry Lee, was still seated at her desk when we walked in. "Jimmy, what do you want?" she asked.

"I want to talk to you about Jerry Lee," I answered pointing to my cousin whose eyes and nose were both running.

"Do you know how many F's he got?" she asked.

"Yes ma'am," I said. "I counted them. There's twenty-seven. But he knows the material."

"But, Jimmy," she said. "He was never here when we gave the tests. He was always absent."

"I know," I said shrugging my shoulders, "but that's because his parents had to move so much. He really knows the material."

She looked skeptical at my suggestion. "Don't you know the material?" I asked Jerry Lee who was standing in the doorway sniffling.

He nodded. "Man, I can't go home with this report card," he said with a grim look on his face, "my folks'll kill me."

"That's right," I chimed in. "If he goes home with this report card, they'll kill him. You don't know his parents."

Mrs. West appeared concerned over our dire predictions for Jerry Lee's life. Taking the report card from him, she studied it for a few moments.

"This is really going against my better judgment," she said reluctantly, "but maybe I could do something."

Finally she reached for an ink eraser and began changing most of the F's to D's. We thanked her profusely and dashed for home. Jerry Lee had passed to the fourth grade in spite of his rec-ord-setting twenty-seven F's, but only with my help.

That summer of 1944 my grandmother's prayer life began touching me for the first time. Some of her results almost rivaled those of the prophet Elijah.

One day Pa Swaggart, who had a small ten-acre farm outside of town, came in from the fields. There was a drought in progress. It hadn't rained in weeks and his ten acres of cotton were burning up. The crop did not need much rain, but it had received none.

"Ada," he said slowly, "I'm not going to make a thing in this world. That cotton is just burning up."

She looked up from her work in the kitchen. "Well, if I pray for rain and if it rains, would you pay your tithes?"

"If it rains, and I make some cotton, sure, I'll pay some tithes."

"Well," she replied, "take me down to the preacher's house."

They drove down to Brother Culbreth's house

and Nannie went in. "Pastor," she said, "I came to pray. My husband said if he makes a good cotton crop, he'll pay tithes." That motivated Brother Culbreth to get down on his knees with Nannie. The church needed tithes almost as much as the cotton needed rain.

Because of the drought the water from the wells had gone bad, too. It was filled with so many minerals it looked like lemonade. People were having to boil the water and then spoon off a thick scum that rose to the top. Thus, the only way to get decent water for cooking or washing clothes was by catching rain water in barrels. In faith, Nannie went home and began to wash out the barrels, getting them ready for the rain she had prayed for.

A neighbor saw Nannie working over the barrels. "Mrs. Swaggart, what are you doing?"

"I've prayed for rain," Nannie said. "I believe it's going to come."

The woman laughed. There wasn't a cloud in the sky and heat waves were rising off the parched Louisiana soil. Yet Nannie continued until she had sufficiently cleaned the barrels.

That night it rained. Not just an hour or two, but all night. The next morning the rain barrels were filled and Pa took Nannie by the hand, repeating his promise to tithe the income from the cotton. He kept his promise.

4
RUNNING
FROM THE CALL

The year the war was over a giant flood spilled over the levees along the Mississippi River. The water backed up along the numerous tributaries that feed the mammoth river creating a backwater many have never forgotten. We were helpless to stop the rising water in the street as it came up on our steps and into our house on Tyler Road. We had no choice but to move across the levee that ringed Lake Concordia and live in a tent city with hundreds of others.

41

Cars stalled in the streets and were abandoned. Motor boats took over and ran up and down Ferriday's main streets. The once fashionable King Hotel—completed in 1927 when another disastrous flood came—was once again severely damaged.

Mama, daddy and Jeanette were unhappy about the move, while I was thrilled. Living in a tent was my idea of having fun. In fact, we were still living in the makeshift tent city when World War II ended in Europe several weeks later.

My folks took a terrific financial loss that year, as did thousands of other families, but it didn't dissuade daddy from encouraging me to develop my piano talent. They signed me up in a piano class taught by the local band director.

I couldn't stick it out, however. The teacher was a stickler for playing "by the book." That was a bore. I'd sit and plunk, plunk, plunk on the piano but it didn't have any life. Playing by the book was a waste of time. I quit after four lessons.

Jerry Lee quit soon afterwards. One afternoon after school I stopped by the teacher's house waiting on Jerry Lee to finish his lesson.

"No, no, you don't play it like that," the teacher admonished. "You play it like this." He proceeded to show Jerry Lee how it should be played by the book.

Jerry Lee was hot-tempered, and he muttered an obscenity thinking the teacher couldn't hear him over the piano. But suddenly the teacher stopped. He looked hard at Jerry Lee. Impulsively he slapped him across the face. That was Jerry Lee's last lesson.

Aunt Rene's son Mickey, was also part of our activities, but he wasn't quite the daredevil Jerry Lee was. Sometimes we'd ride our bicycles down to the Mississippi River bridge at Natchez and walk across. Jerry Lee would climb out on the edge of the bridge and wave at the passing motorists while hanging several hundred feet above the water. If he had fallen, he would have been killed, something we had never considered.

Jerry Lee never really got involved with the church prayer meetings as Mickey, Sullivan, an other cousin David Beatty, and I did. But each time the church held a revival, a morning prayer meeting was held to keep the revival fueled up spiritually.

Back during the summer of 1944 our little church was having another revival, and a morning prayer meeting had begun at Aunt Rene's house. It was a daily occurrence for the four of us to meet with Nannie and Aunt Rene for prayer. From those prayer services, I knew God had called me to preach and one day I would be an evangelist.

Few of the people in church knew anything about the gifts of the Spirit. What we did know had been explained by Brother Culbreth. It was during one of those early prayer meetings the

Lord gave me the gifts of prophecy, and interpretation of tongues.

The first time the Lord spoke through me prophetically I didn't know what was happening. I felt like I was standing outside my body. Then I began to describe exactly what I saw ". . . a powerful bomb destroying an entire city . . . tall buildings crumbling . . . people screaming." I didn't know it then, but there wasn't a bomb available with the power I described.

Word spread about the strange goings-on at Aunt Rene's. People from all over town came, filling up her living room. Soon the crowd was so large we moved to the little white frame church. Still the prophecies came forth. People were captivated by the prophecy on the bomb, which came almost daily.

"The prophecies weren't given particularly loud," daddy remarked to the pastor one day after church, "but a person could hear in front of the church just as plainly as in the back."

"That's true," agreed Brother Culbreth. "You know, that's really normal. Jesus spoke to thousands of people at a time, and he never used a microphone or a loudspeaker."

Many outsiders, who wandered into the little church on Texas Street, were saved after hearing the prophecies. Others, feeling convicted, left. Some dismissed the whole matter because I was only nine years old. But a year later, when the two Japanese cities of Hiroshima and Nagasaki were destroyed by an atomic blast, nobody thought the prophecies were childish any more.

Increasingly as I prayed in the little woods behind the house and read my Bible, I felt the hand of God on my life. Where He would lead, I did not know.

By the time I had reached thirteen, the other boys whom I had grown up with—Jerry Lee, Mickey, Sullivan and David—were no longer interested in church or the things of God. I was basically the only young person my age trying to live for the Lord. We would all get together and talk. But later they would leave and go to the movies. It became a lonely, dreary time. I was constantly plagued with thoughts I was missing out on life.

Finally the pressure got to me and I went to daddy. He and mama were resting on the bed that Saturday afternoon. I hadn't been to a movie in five years.

"Daddy, do you think it would be okay for me to take in a movie this afternoon?" I asked. "All the guys are going."

He was reading the town's weekly newspaper, but looked up as I spoke. He was crying. So was mama. Obviously their commitment to God was much deeper than I suspected. They had surely noticed that I was not the "spiritual boy" I had once been. My request had wounded them.

I stood for what seemed like an eternity. Daddy never said a word. Finally I walked out of the house and went to the movies with my cousin, Mickey. But I was sick about it the moment I sat down in the dark theater. Halfway through the movie, I got up abruptly and stumbled out into the afternoon sunshine.

I was confused and bewildered. My insides were aching. But I was afraid to ask God to forgive me, for that would mean confessing something was wrong in my life. I put my Bible in a dresser drawer. I no longer went outside to my prayer altar behind the house. Miserable, I had just enough religion to keep me from overt sin, but not enough to give me any joy.

The next step was predictable. I tried to see how deep in sin I could slide. Jerry Lee and I began breaking into local stores and stealing. Little things at first, but planning, always planning for a big heist. The next day we would go by the police station and ask if they knew anything about the robbery.

Mr. Harrison, a pleasant gray-haired man in his early fifties, had replaced Pa Swaggart as police chief. "No," he would say, "we haven't caught 'em yet but we're on their trail right now."

"How many do you figure are involved?" we would ask.

"Oh, it's a gang, at least," he would say with great assurance.

It was a lark to us. We thought we had put one over on the law. I couldn't count the times we walked off laughing after one of those talks with Mr. Harrison. We even stole some scrap iron from Uncle Lee's own backyard and then sold it back to him. Uncle Lee had often boasted nobody ever "took him" in a business deal. But Jerry Lee and I had.

One dreary, cold night we broke into a warehouse on the outskirts of town only to find it filled with barbed wire, rolls of it. "Well, let's go," Jerry Lee said disgustedly, "there's nothing here but this dumb barbed wire."

"No," I answered firmly, "we've got to take some of it."

Jerry Lee put his hands on his hips and looked at me strangely. "What in the name of heaven are we going to do with barbed wire?" he asked.

"Well, this job is wasted if we don't take something," I said kicking a roll of the cantankerous wire.

But the game ended when one night I didn't go with Jerry Lee and he got caught. The trip cost Uncle Elmo several hundred dollars to get Jerry Lee out of jail. Maybe the police weren't so dumb after all. We decided to forget a life of crime. It was too risky for such little money.

I guess running isn't very exciting when you're running in the wrong direction. At times, alone in my room, I actually prayed, "Lord, please leave me alone. I don't want to preach."

I no longer considered myself a Christian. I refused to attend church unless daddy forced me. Mama, daddy and Nannie were heartbroken over me. They knew God had called me to the ministry and they continued praying for me.

"God has called you," Nannie would remind me in a gentle way, "and you're going to follow Him. You can be sure of it."

I knew my running from God was hurting Nannie. She seemed to have such hope in me. She never reprimanded me but always appeared calm and sure that I would follow God. That by itself was a powerful drawing force.

For months I tried to drown myself in activity—playing the piano and boxing. My goal was to become the heavyweight champion of the world. Actually my father had had the same desire when he was younger, but during an exhibition match at the local American Legion hall, a first-round punch on his glass jaw laid him out cold. That was the end of his boxing career.

Like daddy, the avenue of boxing closed on me one day. I had taken up the sport because I wanted to be strong and powerful. In reality, I was slim and thin. All of the school's athletes were required to take a preliminary physical. The doctor examining me looked strange after placing his stethoscope near my heart. He placed the cold instrument there again.

"What's the matter?" I asked looking down at his furrowed brow.

"Your heart is beating fast," he replied tersely. "Have you been running or something?"

"No," I answered. "How fast is it beating?"

"Over a hundred times a minute," he responded.

"What's normal?" I questioned as an uneasy feeling began to settle on me.

"Seventy to eighty."

"Well, what can I do about it?" I asked.

He looked at me seriously. "I'm sorry to tell you this," he said, "but I can't approve you to participate in any sports for school. If I did, this rapid heartbeat might become fatal."

"Fatal." The word seemed to be driven into my heart.

The new high school had just been built on the Clayton highway and I walked upstairs to the locker room to be alone. I was crushed. For several minutes I stood looking out a window trying to overcome the disbelief. I had had no idea anything was wrong with me. Now I was ruled out of all sports. My plans for becoming a boxer were dashed in one blow.

Across the treetops and houses, I could see the tiny steeple of the little Assembly of God church two miles away. Tears came to my eyes as I reflected on all the times I had spent there with mama, daddy and Nannie. Memories of all the times praying at Aunt Rene's came to my mind. Somehow I knew I was being forced to obey God.

"God," I cried, still looking out the window, "everything I try to do you stop me. It looks like I'm going to have to preach in spite of everything I want to do." I turned away from the window as several boys walked in.

"What's wrong?" one of them asked me.

"Nothing," I wiped the tears quickly from my eyes.

I walked home that afternoon heartbroken. Finding mama, I sat down and began explaining the situation to her. She always seemed to have an ear for me.

"Well Jimmy, God has a way of turning us around," she said softly. Her words bit into my heart. "Especially," she continued, "when we start going the wrong way."

I knew she was right. My plans hadn't included the Lord and I knew He was allowing me to be stopped—but why me? Couldn't He get anybody else to preach?

5
THE ANOINTING
OF THE DEVIL

There was an elderly black man in town everybody called Old Sam. I doubt he'd ever been to school a day in his life but he was one of the greatest piano players I'd ever heard. Old Sam did odd jobs around town and whenever we could, we got him over to our house to play. He did tunes like "Shanty Town," "Harbor Lights," and "St. Louis Blues." He played with such swinging rhythm it stirred something deep inside me. How I longed to play like that.

In piano playing, the left hand is one of the most difficult arts to master, and that was Old Sam's specialty. Jerry Lee and I were literally hypnotized by what we called Sam's walking left hand. It seemed to dance over the keys.

Many times we sat for hours listening to Old Sam play. He never actually sat down and taught us. But we could watch what he was doing and learn it. Jerry Lee and I both began to develop our left hands to play somewhat as Old Sam did. We were together every day and playing the piano most of the time. In fact, the keys on Jerry's piano ultimately wore down to the wood and turned swayback like an old, worn-out mule. My upright piano wasn't worn that much even though he and I were constantly playing it. I played the bass and Jerry Lee would do the treble at the same time. For a little added spice, we crossed our hands in the middle.

Occasionally we would both break down and go to church—but only to play the piano. The folks always requested us to play church favorites such as "Jesus Hold My Hand," "Just a Little Talk with Jesus," "Keep on the Firing Line" and the like. We always managed to work in Old Sam's rhythm pattern. The people always loved it, but the pastor didn't like that rhythm.

"You can play in church any time you want," he admonished us after one service, "but don't play it with that rhythm. I won't have it."

Unwanted, we began participating in the talent shows in the area. They were held at the schools and anyone could enter. Singing, dancing, playing instruments, even such novelties as playing the spoons were all considered talent.

Most of the time we played double pianos. After a while we had won so many of these contests the judges wouldn't allow us to enter any more. "If you do we know who's going to win," the judges remarked after a show, "so there's no need letting you play."

But one night we played in a talent show over in Jonesville where only adults were allowed to compete. The show was for dance bands and singers—people who made their living in the business. They agreed to let us enter because of our reputation, even though we were only in our early teens.

Instead of allowing us to play together though, the judges permitted us to do one song apiece. It was a good thing my back was turned to the crowd of several hundred because I had a first-class case of stage fright.

I had only played a few bars of "Drinking Wine Spo-Dee O'Dee," a song we had heard Old Sam play frequently, when this strange feeling came over me. I was able to do runs on that piano I hadn't been able to do before. It seemed like a force beyond me had gripped and charged my body. My fingers literally flew over the keys.

For the first time in my life, I sensed what it felt like to be anointed by the devil. I don't know any way to describe it. It was unlike anything I had ever experienced in my life. I knew it wasn't from God.

The huge crowd filling that auditorium stood up and cheered wildly. People screamed and whistled. Applause filled the air. I could sense that strange power rushing over me. A chill flickered up my back.

I was scared. Although backslidden, I remembered what I had promised the Lord years before, that I would never play for the world.

After I finished, Jerry Lee sang and played, drawing the identical response from the crowd. That same demonic anointing I experienced was also on him.

Jerry Lee's mother and father drove us back to Ferriday that night, and they were ecstatic about the show. "Did you see those people?" Aunt Mamie asked as the car roared along the black-topped road.

"You bet I did," Uncle Elmo answered. "I've never seen a crowd come to life like that. We've got two rising stars on our hands."

Everybody was happy except me. I was slumped down in the back seat. The crowd's reaction seemed to fill a temporary need in my life, but I was worried. "What am I going to do now?" I pondered. "I won't preach and I won't play in a night club."

A few months later Jerry Lee opened at the Wagon Wheel, a night club over in Natchez. It wasn't a question my cousin had to reflect over. And his parents readily encouraged him in that direction. To them it wasn't a question of sin. It was just another step along the way until Jerry Lee made it into the big time.

The deeper Jerry Lee got into the night club circuit, the more I drew back. On Saturdays, I worked for Pa Swaggart who was operating a grocery store with daddy on the corner of Mississippi and Fourth Avenues. I was behind the meat counter one afternoon scattering sawdust on the floor when a man came in and asked Pa to see me.

Dressed in blue jeans and bare footed, I walked around the counter to talk with the man. "I own a night club over in Natchez," he explained, adjusting a string tie that seemed uncomfortable in the hot afternoon. "I've heard you play. How about coming to play for me?"

"I go to school," I answered wiping my gritty hands on the soiled store apron. I could feel my heartbeat increasing.

He shook his head. "No problem, you'll just play on Saturday."

"I don't know," I said. Something about this overbearing man with the slicked-down brown hair bothered me.

55

"How much money are you making?" he asked looking around the store.

"Four dollars a day."

"Listen," he said sharply, "I'll pay you four times that much. All you have to do is play a couple of hours on Saturday night. How 'bout it?"

I looked over at Pa Swaggart. He was leaning across the meat counter, listening intently. He quickly began adjusting pans of meat inside the counter. The store was quiet. A light afternoon breeze jiggled the screen door. Several cars swished past the store.

I dropped my head. I wanted to shout yes so badly. But I couldn't. Twisting my apron in my fingers I finally looked up, and shook my head.

"Why?" he asked, obviously annoyed.

"I don't know," I answered, my voice trailing off, "I just don't know. But I can't do it."

I turned and ran into the back room crying. I wouldn't be good, yet I couldn't be bad. All I knew was I had made a promise to God, and I was afraid to break it.

6
FRANCES

Eddy Arnold and Roy Acuff were the best-known singers in country music and Jerry Lee and I listened to them constantly over the radio. Sometimes we let our dreams run away with us as we talked of leaving Ferriday for the bright lights of New York, Los Angeles or Nashville. We wanted to be any place but Ferriday.

Mickey had developed into a fine musician, and Jerry Lee suggested we form a trio. "I'm not interested," Mickey answered when the idea was brought up. "I'll play with you guys in church, but I'm not interested in leaving town and playing in clubs."

Aunt Rene's strong influence was still working in Mickey's life. Actually mama and daddy tried to keep me in line but I had wild ideas. If you told me I couldn't do something, I would die trying to do exactly that.

When Jerry Lee was home the two of us worked constantly trying to perfect a stage act in which both of us played the piano. He did the singing. His full, strong voice had an almost magnetic effect on people. They were drawn to him as if by some supernatural power.

But our dreams to leave Ferriday somehow seemed to always elude our grasp. Jerry Lee was playing on the weekends, but we never left Ferriday together. We seemed chained to the place.

"I don't understand it," I told him one day, "every time we get ready to leave something comes up."

"It really gets me," he answered. "It's almost like something is blocking our way. I wonder if that's the case?"

That question remained unanswered for many months. Our plans for leaving Ferriday were never realized. For some reason, neither of us ever considered leaving town alone.

I didn't discover, until years later, that mama

was spending hours of her time asking God to block my path. She knew God had something better for me, far better.

Jerry Lee's life style, from the time he began playing in nightclubs, seemed to keep him in trouble. His parents finally decided to send him to a Bible school at Waxahachie, Texas. Perhaps, they hoped, that would straighten him out.

"This is Jerry's last chance," Aunt Mamie said the morning Jerry Lee and several other boys left for Texas.

But three months later, Jerry Lee was back home. "They wouldn't let me play piano in chapel," he explained to me, "so I just left."

The truth of the matter was Jerry Lee played songs in chapel the same way he had been playing in night clubs. The school's teachers were outraged, and refused to let him continue.

Things were different in our home. Daddy had begun traveling and preaching revivals. He went into several isolated areas where there was no full-gospel church, and helped the people construct a building and start a congregation. He was a good preacher and attracted big crowds from the start. But his music was even better than his preaching. Both he and mama were excellent musicians and singers, and my sister Jeanette played the accordion. Even Jerry Lee went along to play.

They constantly begged me to join them. "We need you on the piano," daddy said. But I hated going to the services. Sometimes I would play poorly just to annoy people. Other times, when I sensed the crowd was enjoying the music, I would show off. And on top of it all, daddy's preaching always seemed pointed at me, and I would leave the services miserable.

Often, late at night or in the early morning hours, after mama and daddy had driven for hours to get home from a service out of town, mama would slip into my room where I was sleeping. I would not open my eyes when she kissed me on the cheek, but after she left, I would remember the prayer she had whispered over me. Many nights I would lay awake for hours, crying.

Daddy's grocery business was successful. He bought Pa's ten acres and built a new home there. We were financially comfortable. Yet, somehow, I felt something was going to happen to disrupt things. It did.

In the spring of 1951, mama and daddy called me into the living room. Jeanette, who was now ten years old, was already seated.

"Jimmy," he began, addressing himself to me, "I've called you and Jeanette in here to explain something to you." My heart tensed. I almost knew the pins were going to be knocked out from under me.

"I've decided to sell the business and the house," he said, "I'm going full-time in the ministry."

I knew it! I knew something like this would happen. I began to cry—partly in anger. "Please don't, daddy," I pleaded. "You've already got a church at Hebert. You can continue working and pastor the church, too. You just can't give all of this up."

"Jimmy," he said kindly, "the Lord has told me to make this step. I have no choice but to obey."

"But, dad . . . ."

"No, son. If I stay here the business will demand my time. I know it will. Money has been one of my problems and I'm determined to have victory over it."

The thought of daddy going full-time into the ministry was absolute torture for me. For years after that, when I had to fill out a school form listing my parents' occupation, I left it blank. I detested the thought of him being in the ministry. I didn't want to be a PK—a preacher's kid. I didn't want to hear any more about God or church. I wanted to be left alone—to live my life my way.

Within the month, though, daddy turned the Hebert church over to another preacher and he opened tent services in Wisner, thirty miles north of Ferriday. Many nights Jerry Lee went up to play the piano and sing for the services. Even Aunt Rene joined in the singing. There were large crowds. Daddy decided to build a church there.

"Oh, God," I thought when daddy announced his plans for Wisner, "that has got to be the worst place in the world." I had passed through the little community before. Ferriday was small, but it looked huge compared to Wisner. He could have picked any place but Wisner.

But people were immediately attracted to the Wisner Assembly of God. Many were saved and filled with the Holy Spirit. The church building went up in three months. The ministry was flourishing.

Then one afternoon Jeanette came home from the services and announced, "I saw the prettiest girl in church today."

"I ain't interested in girls," I shouted, running her out of my room.

I had never had time for girls. I was either playing the piano or trying to make money. I shot pool, rolled dice, anything to make money. While smoking, drinking and movies were—to me—sinful, I saw nothing wrong with gambling. Most of the time, I would gamble half the night and sleep during the day.

But ultimately I decided to attend the church in Wisner and check on this pretty girl Jeanette kept talking about.

Sitting in the back, Jeanette started nudging

me. "There she is on the first row in the choir."

My eyes scanned the choir's first row settling on a girl in a white blouse. "Third from the end?" I asked Jeanette.

"Yeah."

I looked again. Jeanette was right. This was the prettiest girl I had ever seen. Her dark brown hair was long and rich looking. The puffy sleeves on her blouse seemed to add even more beauty to her natural good looks.

"What's her name?"

"Frances Anderson. She lives in Wisner."

Mama and daddy had always complained about my appearance. I was a sloppy dresser. I wouldn't comb my hair. Being almost like corn silk, it was difficult to comb and make stay. Once I got mad and told Jerry Lee to cut it.

"Man, I don't know anything about cutting hair," he said.

"That's all right with me," I answered. "It can't look any worse."

But immediately after seeing Frances Anderson, I decided it was time to start sprucing up. Jerry Lee, on the other hand, had always been the Beau Brummell of Ferriday. Now it was my turn.

It didn't take me long to get acquainted with Frances Anderson, and it wasn't long before we were sitting in church together. Frances had an older brother and two younger sisters. They lived about two miles from Wisner on a forty-acre farm. Thus when daddy and mama finally decided to move to Wisner, I accepted it with grace. I knew it would allow me more time with Frances.

Instead of continuing in high school, however, I dropped out. I was seventeen years old and just didn't feel it was important. Actually I had given up on school several years before, but continued going just to appease mama and daddy. Most of the time had been spent in study hall reading books.

Frances' parents were against us dating but I was able to talk her mother into it. Her parents were concerned about her getting involved with me. They held a poor opinion of Pentecostals, though they went to church infrequently and knew very little about them.

Frances had an uncle who attended daddy's church. He had kidded her from the beginning about me. "You're going to wind up marrying that preacher's son," he told her.

"That's not true," Frances snapped the first time her uncle mentioned me. But we could see, after three months had passed, we were making plans to get married even though we were still teenagers.

I still had problems, an explosive temper, a rebellious attitude toward everybody and a bad case of jealousy when it came to Frances. Even after I bought the marriage license I kept it thirty days before we ever used it. Actually I had lied about both of our ages to even get the license.

Frances had even told me one day she didn't know if she could live with me and all my problems. Yet, we still talked about getting married, as if we were being guided by some unseen force. The situation seemed to be moving so rapidly that I couldn't stop it. And I wouldn't have stopped it if I could.

Mama and daddy weren't opposed to the marriage but they wanted to be sure I knew what I was getting into. "Do you realize what you're doing?" mama asked one day.

Before I could answer, daddy interrupted. "How are you going to make a living?" I was only doing odd jobs at the time and had no steady source of income.

"The world's too big for me not to be able to make a living," I cockily answered.

They were not convinced. In fact, daddy refused to marry us because Frances' parents wouldn't give their consent. We had no choice but to ask a local Baptist pastor, whose daughter was a friend, to perform the ceremony. I borrowed mama's ring one Friday night and we were married in a quiet home ceremony. Afterwards I took Frances home and I went to mine.

The next day I went out to explain the situation to Mr. and Mrs. Anderson. Frances' mother was the only one home and I briefly explained that we had gotten married the night before. The room was deathly silent as I spoke. To say she was upset was putting it mildly. All her plans for Frances finishing school and going on to college had been torpedoed by one wild son of a Pentecostal preacher.

Frances and I moved in temporarily with mama and daddy until I could find work. It was a frustrating time. At night, when daddy held devotions for the family, I refused to go. People in the church were constantly asking me to play the piano and that made things worse. The one time in my life when I should have been the happiest, I was the most miserable.

In the meantime I got a job as a swamper on a dragline. My job was to supply the oil and grease for the dragline. Dirt and grime quickly became a way of life. I was seventeen and doing a man's work. Yet it was all the work I could find and I lived with a fear the boss would fire me because I was too young.

It was this fear which drove me back to God. "I'll stop this running," I promised, "and I'll come back to you, if you'll let me keep this job."

That same afternoon, the superintendent came out to where I was working. "There's no problem," he announced, "you can work on."

Relieved, I slacked off on my part of the promise. No need to go back to God now. I had a good job. Two weeks later, the superintendent

66

was back. "I'm sorry," he said, "we can't keep you on the job. You're underage."

In January, 1953, Vincent Roccaforte, the evangelist whose ministry had touched my parents years before, came to Wisner for services. The revival began on a Sunday. I don't remember the sermon but I do remember, on Monday night, sitting in the back making a mental list of all the things I would have to do if I came back to the Lord. I would have to go to church every time the doors opened. I would have to quit shooting pool. I would have to give up the movies. I would have to give up some of my ideas for making money. I might even have to go to the youth rallies. The last was the worst of all. I hated those meetings.

But the pressure of God was greater than my fear of losing my freedom. On the way to the altar I made a promise to the Lord. "Lord, I'll even go to those dumb rallies if I have to."

I fell down down at the altar and begged God's forgiveness. For the first time in four years, I felt clean again. The dull ache in my heart was gone. My head was clear of confusion.

When I stood up from the altar, I caught a glimpse of mama walking back and forth on the platform praising God. She rushed over to me throwing her arms around me as we wept together. Daddy came forward and knelt at the altar for a long time in tears.

Two nights later, Nannie and Pa came up from

Ferriday for the services. "I knew it!" she responded when told I came back to the Lord. "There was nothing else that could be done. I never doubted it. The Lord told me a long time ago you were coming back."

I didn't have the heart to tell her I was already having second thoughts. In fact, I was beginning to think of ways I could get out of my renewed commitment to God. I knew I could probably handle mama and daddy. That was easy. But Nannie was another matter entirely.

A sinking feeling lodged in my stomach as I heard her talk. She sounded so positive. "I'm locked into this," I conceded to myself. "It's hopeless. I'm going to have to follow God anyway."

Having lost the job on the dragline, I was back to odd jobs. Hauling gravel, chopping cotton, anything to get food on the table. Finally Pa asked me to come down to Ferriday and help him once again at the store. While I was back in Ferriday, Frances and I began attending a revival in Natchez at an Assembly of God church.

It was a very informal meeting. People would run up and down the aisles shouting. The preacher would pray for people and they would fall on the floor under the power. Many nights the aisles were lined with prostrate people slain in the Spirit. Yet in the midst of all the excess, God was moving.

I had been gloriously filled with the Holy Spirit as a child. But four years of wandering from God had left me bereft of the Spirit. What I once possessed had been lost. Maybe I had lost it through disobedience, but whatever, I needed it back.

As the meetings progressed in Natchez, I became so hungry I felt I would do anything just to receive a refilling of the Holy Spirit. Frances was not at all anxious and was easily filled. I had earnestly sought God without success. Frances was speaking in tongues and gloriously happy. "It's not fair," I thought, "I'm seeking too."

The revival ended in Natchez without me being refilled, even though I had been fasting and praying daily. I guess it was difficult for me because I had been so rebellious against God. Then, services began in Ferriday with Brother Gilliam and I began seeking all over again.

Many people were fasting for me. Many nights after the services ended, we went to someone's house and they prayed for me. "What's wrong with you?" people finally began asking.

I was perplexed. I knew there was more but I didn't know how to get it. I decided to confess everything I had done wrong. I started on Nannie and told her of all the petty thievery Jerry Lee and

I had done several years before. Maybe this was the thing holding me back.

"Do you think I should go to the police and confess it, too?" I asked.

"No," Nannie responded, "I don't think that'll do it. We just need to stand on the promises of God. He says He'll give the Holy Spirit to anyone who asks. Now we're just going to continue asking."

Even though I continued asking, I got nowhere. One night I came home discouraged after another trip to the altar without any visible results. Nannie's brother, John Lewis, was at her house.

"Jimmy," he said sitting down on a bed to talk with me, "I had almost the same thing happen to me. I sought long and hard for God to fill me. But the answer came when I accepted, by faith, what the Bible already said. It's one thing to read it in the Bible. It's an entirely different thing to believe and accept that Word."

Uncle John's talk encouraged me. I felt I wasn't alone. Others had difficulty in receiving the Holy Spirit, also. I knew I had to believe the Word was for me, and accept that Word.

The following night, I once again went to the altar and began praying. Somehow I sensed the Lord starting to move through me. Even though I had close experiences with Him as a child, I still didn't know how to yield to Him.

70

I was lying flat on my back in front of the altar attempting to receive the Holy Spirit. Sister McGlothin, one of the saints of the church, obviously sensed my problem and knelt beside me. "Dear Lord, he's yours," she repeated. "Dear Lord, he's yours."

As she repeated that phrase over and over, something broke within me and a flow began. Somehow in the background I heard Frances, Mickey, David and several others singing, "Jesus Is the Sweetest Name I Know." Then I felt God moving powerfully within me. I felt it coming just as it had when I was a child. It seemed to flow through my heart and I began speaking in tongues. It was truly living water.

Finally I leaped to my feet praising God in a language I had not learned. Everybody was shouting and praising God with me.

I called mama as soon as I got back home. "God's refilled me with the Holy Spirit," I announced excitedly into the phone.

"Oh, I'm so happy," mama said. "Last night I had a dream you died and now I know. You did die—to the things of this world."

7
"SON, YOU'VE GOT THE FIRE"

There was never a waking moment, during those four years I was running from God, that I had forgotten my call to preach. I knew one day it would happen. Once refilled I knew the Lord was ready for me to preach— but I was too scared to begin in church. Six months after I finally surrendered to God, I was praying at the altar one night when I began to receive what I thought was a new direction.

"I've got something I want to do Saturday," I

told Frances when I got back to the pew. "I want you to help me."

"What?" she asked with a puzzled look on her face.

"I'm going to have a street service in Mangham."

"Sure," she said with a grin, "whatever you want me to do."

Frances and mama had frequently talked about the call on my life, and everybody expected me to begin preaching someday.

Mangham, a town with fewer than five hundred people, was the place where daddy was born. Saturday was grocery-buying day for most families. I asked the town's only policeman if I might preach outside a grocery store. He shrugged and told me to go ahead. I was finally "in the ministry."

A small crowd of fifteen or twenty people gathered as we sang, "There Is Power in the Blood." I had my accordion with me and several kids from church had their guitars. Then I started to preach.

"In the fall of 1939, Hitler invaded Poland," I began nervously, and I proceeded to tell the story of World War II and how America was drawn into the picture. I traced the events up to 1953 and concluded that America was in deep sin and under God's judgment.

My hands were trembling, my knees were

shaking, and my collar was wet with sweat, but I kept going. In ten minutes, I preached everything I knew—twice.

Afterwards the burly policeman came up to shake my hand. "Son, you've got the fire," he said patting me on the back. "No question about that."

From that Saturday on, I preached everywhere I could. I was still doing odd jobs and in the afternoons Frances and I would go house-to-house giving out gospel tracts and telling people about Jesus. On Saturdays, we would hit the streets of nearby towns, preaching to whomever would listen. Clayton, Winnsboro, Gilbert, Wisner, Sicily Island, Mangham—all got a taste of my first attempts to preach.

It took me awhile to get up enough courage to preach a street service in Ferriday. I knew too many people there. Yet I knew it was time to take my stand before the hometown folks. People filled up the streets as usual and after that service Fred McCollough walked up to shake my hand. He had been my math teacher at Ferriday High School.

"Son, out of all the boys I had in school," he said sincerely, "you were the last one I ever dreamed would be a preacher."

"I guess you're right, Mr. McCollough," I said, "but that's the difference God really makes in your life. He makes a real change."

The street services became so successful we graduated to a flatbed truck with microphones and loudspeakers. Afterwards we would give out thousands of tracts and walk among the crowd sharing our personal testimonies.

Frances and I saved enough money to buy a small house trailer. We parked it in Aunt Rene's yard in Ferriday. Daddy was building a new church in Vidalia, just ten miles down the road. He was also constructing houses for a living and I worked as an assistant. In the afternoon, I would come in from work, clean up and Frances and I would go over to Nannie's for prayer. It was a daily ritual. We would talk a long time about the things of God before getting on our knees in prayer—for at least an hour.

Daddy let me use his two ton truck to travel around. In fact, we used that truck for street services. But I needed a car of my own. One afternoon I casually mentioned the situation to Nannie.

"Let's pray for some transportation," she suggested.

"Fine," I answered, "I need it."

Nannie went down on her knees beside her favorite chair. I followed and we began praying. "Lord, you know I need some means to get around in," I prayed, "but if you want me to hitchhike I'll gladly do it. If you want me to have nothing, I'll accept it."

After I had prayed like that for a while, I noticed Nannie had quit praying. "Wait a minute," she said gently. "If you keep praying like that you'll never get a car. We're not down here praying to hitchhike. You need some transportation. Now, let's pray positively. In faith!"

I was embarrassed. I had never had anybody to stop me right in the middle of a prayer. But somehow I recognized Nannie was right. I was not praying correctly. I was praying a double-minded prayer, and I knew the Bible said such a man would have a hard time getting his prayers answered.

Within a week I was given a Studebaker truck. God had answered our prayers, once they had been turned in the right direction.

Living around Nannie proved a source of constant inspiration and instruction. Seeing her prayers answered in my childhood—and now in young adulthood—dramatically touched my life. Her positive word always drove away the discouragement I constantly fought. "Don't you believe God for little things?" she asked. "Then why not believe Him for big things . . . for great things. He's not a little God. He's big."

Nannie was right. But I was just a nineteen-year-old kid working part-time odd jobs during the week and preaching wherever I could on the weekends. Not only that but Frances was already expecting a baby and I was beginning to feel the pressure of impending fatherhood. In the shape I was in, it would take a big God's help.

Word trickled into the backwoods of Louisiana that God had raised up some great healing evangelists who were holding large meetings around the nation. Names like Jack Coe, William Branham and Oral Roberts were often on people's lips. Gordon Lindsay's *Voice of Healing* magazine carried reports of what was happening "out there." It whetted my desire to see for myself what God was doing in the world.

Nannie and I practically devoured every issue of the magazine we received. My heart burned as I read of the thousands being saved, healed and filled with the Holy Spirit throughout the world.

Just as Timothy's grandmother Lois built faith into him as a young preacher (II Timothy 1:5), Nannie did the same thing with me. "One day you're going to preach to thousands," Nannie said constantly, "just like in these meetings!" Then she would hold up a copy of the *Voice of Healing*.

But it was too much to believe. I felt so inferior and preaching to those kind of crowds looked impossible. Nannie never doubted, but inside my heart I said, "There's no way that will ever happen."

I doubted what Nannie said partly because I

couldn't get victory over the small things. I wanted to have a calm temperament, but I was fiery and explosive. I was constantly having to ask forgiveness for something I had done heatedly. How could somebody like me preach to thousands when I couldn't control my temper?

I had set standards for myself so high that I couldn't live by them. As a result I fell deeply into condemnation. Gradually I came to think God had a grudge against me because of my constant failings. I didn't realize He sees us, not as we are, but as we shall be.

The voice of the enemy drove me further into discouragement and depression. "God won't forgive you again," voices said, "you've told Him you wouldn't sin again and yet you have." Slowly I was coming to think there was no hope.

Soon the depression began to affect me physically. I couldn't sleep at night. I was losing weight. Finally I went to a doctor. "You're too young to be having problems like this," he said. "Go sit on a creek bank somewhere and fish. You're on the verge of a nervous breakdown."

The next three days and nights were agony. I didn't sleep at all. I barely ate. My nerves were jangled. Months and months of frustration and despair were coming to a head. I tried to read my Bible yet all the words were cold. I tried to pray yet I couldn't reach God. The third night I went outside our trailer and tried to walk down a darkened road in hopes I could exhaust myself enough to sleep.

It was just before dawn when I came back, the darkest time of the night. It's a haunting time, a strange time to be awake and fearful.

I went to bed when I climbed back into our tiny trailer. And for the next few moments I did not know if I was wide awake or dreaming, but suddenly I found myself in an old house with high ceilings. The room I was in had no windows or furniture. A door leading outside was slightly ajar.

Fear welled up inside of me. I knew I was in an evil place. "Oh God," I thought, "let me get out of this place."

Suddenly the door swung open and a hideous-looking beast stood towering over me. He had the body of a bear and the face of a man. The expression on his face was the grisliest I had ever seen. The beast was the picture of evil.

I looked up at him and every ounce of strength drained from my body. I stumbled and sank down to the floor. I was helpless.

The beast looked at me piercingly, as if to say, "I have you now. This is the end for you." He slowly advanced towards me. I looked around for some weapon to use even though I knew the room was bare.

He was almost an arm's length from me now. "In the name of Jesus," words spoke from inside me.

The beast looked stunned. He clutched his head and screamed as if something had struck him. He staggered back as courage built in me. I stood up, pointing a finger at him and repeated the phrase, "In the name of Jesus." He started falling toward the floor and I heard the sound of a dull thud as he hit.

Now I stood over him as he twisted in pain like a wounded snake just felled with a death blow. This time I shouted it: "In the name of Jesus!" Instantaneously, he was swept out the door as I came to myself. When I did, my hands were lifted toward heaven and I was speaking in tongues. I was miraculously freed!

It was the beginning of being taught the power in the name of Jesus. Unknowingly, I was also combating an evil spirit. In the years to come, I knew I would have to master these lessons—for they could mean the difference between life and death.

8
"WHOLE LOTTA SHAKIN' GOING ON"

During the summer of 1954, soil conservation work was underway in Franklin Parish and God answered our prayers for full-time employment by allowing me to go back to work as a swamper. Ellis Dupree, who had been saved under daddy's ministry, was foreman on the job. I enjoyed working under another Christian.

As before, the work was hot and rough but I enjoyed working with the heavy equipment. The job started just in time, because several weeks later

Frances gave birth to a baby boy in Wisner. We named the baby Donnie, in memory of my own brother whose death ultimately led to my parents' salvation.

The job actually became my Bible school. I could handle the chores of oiling and greasing the dragline and still do all of my studying and praying. Many times I would set the stakes for the dragline to dig by and would have nothing else to do until the ditch was completed. I took advantage of that time to read books or walk off into the swamps to pray or preach to the stumps.

I was constantly buying and reading new books. Anything related to Jesus Christ, I read. Sometimes Frances joked she never saw my face at home without a book stuck in front of it. But something inside of me was hungry. I wanted to know about God. I was greatly intrigued with how God used people. *A Man Sent From God,* the story of William Branham, touched me deeply. I began to see it didn't matter if you were not particularly educated or handsome. In fact, God seemed to delight in choosing the weak and foolish things to confound the wise. I was certainly in that category.

Daddy told me that if I wanted to attend a Bible school he would pay for it. I was a high school dropout and the idea had little appeal, so I simply continued working with the dragline and preaching in services whenever I could.

That same year, 1954, a Memphis truck driver by the name of Elvis Presley made a demonstration record for his mother's birthday at an obscure recording studio called Sun Records.

In the months that followed, Elvis Presley's name became a household word. He ushered in a new form of music, rock-and-roll. It was destined to influence the whole world and hold sway over millions of lives, creating a new spiritual dimension to music—a dimension many felt came from the pit of hell. The new music went beyond mere rhythm. It produced a driving, throbbing beat that stirred the sensual nature of man.

Jerry Lee was one of those who would play a vital role in the enormous growth of the popularity of rock-and-roll. Since leaving Bible school, he had married, become a father, and sold sewing machines door-to-door. He even preached for several months as an evangelist. Unfortunately, he never stuck with any of these endeavors long enough to succeed.

He and Mickey had actually been at one of the street services I had preached in Ferriday. They both stood on the outskirts of the crowd that day with tears running down their faces. But neither of them could resist the tug of the world on their lives.

I walked over to talk with them after the service. "I wish I had the guts to do that," Mickey said referring to my preaching.

Jerry Lee attempted to be a little more light-hearted. "Jim, I just want you to know, me and Mickey are going out and hit the big time," he promised grandly, "and help support you in the ministry."

"That's fine, Jerry," I responded, "but you'd do yourself a bigger favor by staying here and going into the ministry with me."

Neither of my cousins said anything else. They stood there for a while and finally slipped away. I knew they had decided to take a different direction. All I could do was pray for them.

Uncle Elmo had heard about Elvis Presley becoming an overnight sensation. He decided to take Jerry Lee to Memphis for an audition with Sam Phillips at Sun Records. They sold eggs to get money for the trip, but when they arrived in Memphis, Sam Phillips wasn't around.

"Well, I had enough money to get here," Jerry Lee announced testily, "and I don't have enough money to get home . . . so somebody's gonna listen to me."

Phillips ultimately showed up and they gave Jerry Lee a test run. The minute his fingers ran across the piano keys an engineer punched Phillips. "I think you've got another Elvis," he exclaimed.

That same day, Jerry Lee recorded an old country tune, "Crazy Arms." Highlighted by his distinctive piano playing and singing, the song was on the pop music charts and selling at a brisk pace within a matter of weeks. In two months, the record passed the 300,000 mark.

I was sitting in a little diner in Winnsboro, while the crew moved the huge dragline into another position, the first time I heard the record. An odd feeling swept through me as I heard the familiar strains of my cousin's voice over the juke box, ". . . Crazy Arms that long to hold somebody new. . . ."

My thoughts drifted back to the times Jerry Lee and I had played piano together, the times we had talked about making lots of money, the times we had planned to leave Ferriday for the big time. Now it looked as if Jerry Lee had finally realized his part of the dream.

But what about me. Here I was, dressed in greasy overalls, my face covered with grime. All I could do was serve and obey. I had no other choice. I had a different master. Dark, cloudy thoughts hung in my mind ". . . I'll never do anything but preach in little backwoods churches . . . grease and grime is really my lot."

Yet deep inside I resolved if that's what God wanted, that's what I would do. I would work on the dragline and preach whenever I could until Jesus came.

I looked around. Practically everybody in the small diner was looking at me. They knew I was Jerry Lee's cousin. They seemed to be saying. "What do you think about that?"

In a way I was happy for him. He and his family had lived a hard life. All sharecroppers do. This was their first real chance to have anything. Yet I couldn't shake the feeling that he had made a big mistake. I wanted him to live for the Lord and I knew he couldn't do that traveling around the country and playing rock-and-roll to howling mobs in some auditorium.

Months later I was driving home when I heard an announcer play Jerry Lee's newest record, "Whole Lotta Shakin' Going On." After the record, the announcer declared, "Jerry Lee Lewis is the hottest name in show business today."

I guess the man was right. That record sold six million copies and Jerry Lee was being heralded as the new king of rock-and-roll. At one time he played for fifty dollars a night. Now he could demand thousands—and get it.

That summer and the one following, I continued working as a swamper and preaching on the weekends wherever a church door would open. It was on a Sunday morning in December, 1957 and I was scheduled to preach for daddy in Wisner, when Jerry Lee drove up in his Cadillac.

He had reached the pinnacle of success. He had appeared on several national television programs.

His picture was on the cover of many trade magazines. His latest recording, "Great Balls of Fire," was number one in the nation. But he didn't seem to want to talk about all that. Instead he wanted to know how I was doing.

Over breakfast, we talked. "Where are you preaching now? How are the services? Are many people getting saved?" he rattled the questions off like a machine gun. He knew I was going full-time into the ministry after the first of the year. I didn't want to preach to him. But he persisted in wanting to talk about the Lord's work. So that's what we did while we were at home, and then all the way to church.

Jerry Lee appeared to be his usual light-hearted self that morning. But later in church he was deeply affected by the Holy Spirit. His face turned ashen. He gripped the pew in front of him so tightly his knuckles turned white, shaking it as he wept and sobbed.

A number of people moved forward that morning to receive the Lord and repent of their sins. Jerry Lee remained in his seat, sobbing. Finally mama went over to pray with him and urge him to come forward. He always seemed to love her better than any of his aunts and uncles and he hugged her neck emotionally. Yet he would not yield to the Holy Spirit's bidding.

We stopped briefly and talked on the church steps after the service. Up to this point, I had not tried to pressure him on the direction of his life, but I knew, now, I had no other choice. When I did I felt an invisible barrier going up between us.

"You know, Jerry," I said fingering the corners of my Bible, "God really loves you and this is still the best way."

He glanced at me and swallowed hard. "Jim, do you remember when we used to sit on a piano stool and talk about the day we were going to drive one of them?" He pointed to his Cadillac shining in the afternoon sun.

I nodded. How well I remembered.

"Well, I've got that one plus three more just as nice," he said.

"That's fine, Jerry."

"Do you remember when we used to talk about making a thousand dollars a day?" he asked nervously fiddling with his string tie.

"Sure I do. We did a lot of dreaming."

"Well, my dream has come true. Sometimes I make ten thousand." He wasn't just boasting. He was stating a fact, yet underneath it all he seemed unhappy. There was something sorrowful about the way he said it.

"I know," I replied softly, "but what if you lose your soul, Jerry?"

It was a deep, soul-searching moment. He walked over to the side railing of the church steps and stood looking down the driveway. When he turned around there were tears on his face.

"I don't sing or play as well as you do," I said seriously, "but what little I have is God's. All of it. Just think what would happen if you gave him all you have."

"I can't," he mumbled almost incoherently, "I just can't."

Tears gathered in my own eyes as he walked off the steps, got in his car and drove out of sight. I knew Jerry Lee had good intentions. But I couldn't believe they would ever be enough to sustain him in the life he had chosen.

My intentions carried me, however, because I was determined they would be God's intentions also. On January 1, 1958 I left the security of my job as a swamper and entered evangelistic work on a full-time basis. It was a decision Frances and I had talked and prayed over a long time. In fact, she and daddy questioned me extensively about the timing of the decision. But the Lord had given me clear direction, and I was willing to step out in faith.

Several times prior to leaving my job, people approached me about playing the piano in various places. Most of them were gospel quartets. The offers always looked glamorous and appealing. But I never felt free to accept them. I had been called to preach the gospel, not play the piano for someone else.

My first revival was with Pastor Jewell Barton in Sterlington, Louisiana. On the fourth night I became deathly sick with pneumonia. Brother Barton took me to a hospital and later mama and daddy had me transferred to a hospital near Winnsboro where I remained for several days. But I seemed to get worse instead of better. Early one morning, I decided to leave, despite the protests of the hospital staff. I staggered home and collapsed into bed, burning up with fever.

During those days in the hospital I had listened to the radio. The air waves were filled with the heavy rock-and-roll beat of Jerry Lee's music. Mickey had just signed a contract with Dot Records and they were predicting big things for him. Another cousin, Carl McVoy, was with the Bill Black Combo and they had a song in the top forty.

The following night Frances took Donnie and went to a prayer meeting. I stayed home resting and reading the Bible.

All of a sudden it seemed the room was sinking, as if it were an elevator going down a shaft, down, down. It seemed as if all the darkened, oppressive forces of hell had been unleashed against me. I was swamped with depression. Dark, gloomy thoughts roamed through my mind.

"Look at you," the voices said. "If your God is so great, why doesn't He heal you? Your situation is worse than ever. You don't have enough money to pay your hospital bill. You can't even pay your house note. You can't put food on the table. What are you going to do? You've quit your job. You have no source of income."

It seemed as if every demon in hell had crawled out to battle with me.

"Look at Jerry Lee," the voices said. "He used to be a preacher but he's gotten smart. Look at Mickey. He tried living for God but now he's smartened up, too. Look at Carl. His dad is a Church of God preacher but Carl got smart. They're really living, and you're dying. Your God can't even heal you." The voices faded, laughing hilariously as they disappeared.

I cried out for God's help. Finally I reached over and picked up my Bible.

It fell open to Joshua 1:9, "Have not I commanded thee? Be strong and of a good courage; be not afraid, neither be thou dismayed: for the LORD thy God is with thee whithersoever thou goest."

The words seemed to stand out as if capitalized. I read the Scripture over and over and as I did a new strength began to flow into me. It was the Word of God to me—"Be strong, . . ."

God's healing power surged through my body. It was like fire in my veins. I sat up on the side of the bed. Finally I stood up. I was a little dizzy at first but then more steady.

"Lord, you're with me," I shouted hoarsely. "I've been sick long enough. I don't know how I'll

93

pay the bills but I trust you to provide. I don't know how you'll take care of me but I trust you to do it. I have done what you told me to do and I'm going to receive my healing."

I began to walk through the little two-bedroom house with my hands uplifted, as I shouted praises to the Lord. I was healed.

Frances and Donnie came home, and stood in the doorway laughing in joy as I walked through the house talking to God.

"Elvis Presley can have 'Hound Dog' if he wants him, but I'll take the Holy Ghost. Jerry Lee can have 'Great Balls of Fire' but I'll take the Holy Ghost and fire. Hallelujah!" It sounded silly but I was healed—and glad of it.

During the sickness I had to cancel what few meetings we had. Once healed, I called my cousin, Gerald Lewis, in Magnolia, Arkansas, asking him to move up the date of our revival with him. During the months that followed we spent as much time on the road as we did at home—traveling from one small church to another then returning home to pray in another meeting—and enough money to pay the bills.

One item that needed considerable prayer was our battered, blue Plymouth which had long since passed the point of service. The car was literally held together with bailing wire, faith and prayer.

Among other things, the car's valves had been

sticking so that when it sat idling the engine clattered madly. I finally took it to a garage.

"It'll take thirty dollars to fix it," announced the grizzled mechanic, rubbing his oil soaked hands on a dirty rag.

"Thirty dollars?" I questioned incredulously.

"That's right, friend," he answered, "you've got a burned valve."

I took it to another mechanic, but his estimate was even higher—fifty dollars!

Now what? I didn't have the money to repair the car and yet I had to have something to drive. That very week I was driving between Wisner and Ferriday every day to preach a revival, sixty miles a day.

It was that week Uncle Elmo had made his pitch for me to go to Memphis. My decision to say "no" seemed even more foolish when I looked at that junk pile I was driving to church. Elijah had a chariot. Ezekiel had a wheel. All I had was a burned out valve.

Driving slowly away from the garage so as not to upset the Plymouth's delicate condition, I turned off the highway down an isolated, dirt road. Light from the afternoon sun crisscrossed the car's hood as it filtered through some nearby shade trees, momentarily reflecting off the silvery hood ornament. A light spring breeze danced through the leaves.

Prayer was my only weapon. If God could heal

my sick body, surely He could repair my sick car. It was all the same to Him.

The foolishness of the situation caused me to chuckle. Was I really dumb enough to ask God to heal a car?

"Devil," I announced impulsively, "if you think I've been crazy before, just listen to this. I'm going to ask the Lord to heal this Plymouth."

Feeling lightheaded and a little giggly, I got out of the car, walked around to the front and poured some oil on the silver ornament—oil from a little bottle I carried in my pocket to anoint the sick. Oil ran down the front of the old Plymouth as I prayed fervently.

"Lord, you know what the situation is with this car. The mechanics say the engine is practically burned up. I desperately need this car to get to my revival meetings. So I'm asking you in Jesus' name to heal this car . . . and I'm thanking you for it right now."

"You're an idiot," a voice whispered in my ears as I walked back around the car looking at the oxidized paint finish and the window glass turning cloudy around the corners.

Back behind the wheel, I mashed the Plymouth's starter, kicking over the engine, purr-r-r-r-r. "Man," I thought to myself, "this thing runs like a new Singer sewing machine."

"Praise God," I shouted. "Thank you, Jesus!"

I drove that Plymouth for several months

without a problem before selling it. I warned the new owner of a possible problem with the valves but he was a shade tree mechanic and said he knew how to handle any such problem if it arose.

Weeks later I saw him. "How's the Plymouth?" I asked wondering if the car was still in one piece.

"Nothing's wrong with it," he answered. "I checked the valves. They're perfect." The valves didn't stick but the healing did.

The Ferriday meeting stretched into a second week, but the devil fought me every day of that revival. I had already turned down the biggest promoter in the United States, and yet the struggle continued.

Jerry Lee's parents had been attending the services and one night they invited us to spend a night with them at their newly purchased home. "Look there, Jim," Uncle Elmo remarked as we drove up after the service. "Count those cars."

Five of the most expensive cars in the world were parked in the front yard—Lincolns, Cadillacs and one or two I didn't recognize. There must have been $50,000 worth of cars parked under the willow trees.

"They belong to Jerry," Uncle Elmo said. "He drives one when he gets tired of the rest."

Frances helped Aunt Mamie with supper while I went into Jerry Lee's room to change clothes. When you have a summer—winter—fall—spring suit all rolled into one, you learn to take special care of it.

When I sat down on the bed to take off my shoes, I noticed the closet door was ajar. My curiosity got the best of me. I opened the door. It contained rows of suits belonging to my cousin and endless boxes of shoes, some opened, others seemingly never touched. And these were just his clothes when he came home to Ferriday. He had another supply in Memphis.

I looked at my entire wardrobe lying on the bed—one suit. I had been offered several suits from a man back in Arkansas but they wouldn't fit so I was stuck with the twenty dollar Stein. I had one pair of shoes to go with the outfit.

"Living for God doesn't pay very well," a voice whispered.

My thoughts were interrupted by Aunt Mamie knocking on the door. "I've got something to tell you Jimmy," she announced happily.

"What's that?"

"Jerry Lee called tonight. He's just signed a new contract," she replied with a dreamy look in her eyes. "He'll be getting twenty-five hundred dollars a show. I can't even imagine that kind of money."

She closed the door and I stood, locked in my own thoughts. I had forgotten about the pastor putting the offering in my coat pocket that night, but as I changed clothes I found it, folded up in a dollar bill. I spread it out on the bed. A single dollar bill, some nickels, dimes and a few quarters. Two dollars and fifty cents. The world pays $2500.00—God's servants get $2.50.

"Living for God sure gives small pickings," the voice returned.

"Where are you, O Lord?" But God seemed to be a million miles away. I was going to have to work through this problem by myself.

"Lord," I said, "I can't feel your Spirit and it doesn't seem like you're anywhere around here. But I just want you to know I'm going to preach your word if I have to patch my suits and put pasteboard in my shoes. I'm going to serve you. I don't care what happens."

Apparently that was just what God wanted me to say, to commit myself once again. Maybe it was some kind of test and God wanted to know where my allegiance was. As Job said about the Lord "though he slay me, [or starve me] yet will I trust him."

Suddenly God's presence exploded in the room. A joy began filling my soul and flowing through me as I felt the warmth of the Holy Spirit spilling over me like a waterfall. I began to weep—and shout. "Glory!! Hallelujah!! God reigns!! He is God. The Lord is God of the universe!! And I am His!!!"

I broke out of the bedroom still weeping and shouting.

"What in the world went on in that bedroom?"

Aunt Mamie asked as I sat down at the supper table.

"It was just me and the Lord getting together," I answered as the joy continued bubbling up within me.

"Glory! Praise the Lord!" The waterfall started again as I sat at the table shouting.

I rejoiced inside. "Why do I need forty suits, I'm clothed in a robe of righteousness! Why do I need Cadillacs and Lincolns when I can ride with the King of Kings? Jerry Lee can go to Sun Records in Memphis, I'm on my way to heaven with a God who supplies all my need according to His riches in glory by Christ Jesus." I didn't know how to explain it, but I knew I had won a great victory over the powers of darkness. God had encouraged me in spite of all the circumstances when I renewed my commitment. My commitment to the Lord had to be renewed daily. When I did, I learned how to have continual victory over the enemy.

Cousins, Jimmy Swaggart (left) and Jerry Lee Lewis, 1961 at Clayton, Louisiana. One of Jerry Lee's gold records is on the wall behind.

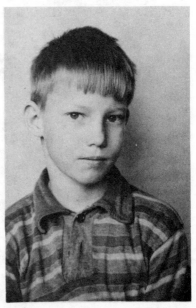

Jimmy Swaggart at age nine, 1944, about the time of the atomic bomb prophecies.

Main street–Ferriday, Louisiana, 1976.

The Reverend W.L. Swaggart, Jimmy's father, 1976.

The little white frame Assembly of God church, Ferriday, Louisiana.

The tractor-trailer rig that carries the team's equipment to its many engagements around the nation.

Jimmy Swaggart preaching in a crusade.

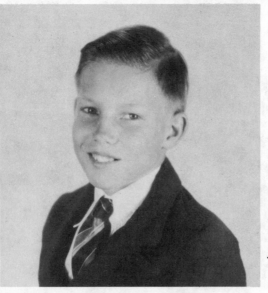

Jimmy dressed for church, age twelve, about 1947.

104

The Swaggart family about 1943. From left to right are Jimmy, W.L., Minnie Bell, and Jeanette.

A typical Jimmy Swaggart crusade.

Frances, Donnie and Jimmy Swaggart, 1966.

Jimmy taping the first "Camp Meeting Hour" program, 1969.

The church in Wisner where he found Frances. 1957.

A skinny, young preacher–Jimmy Swaggart. 1958.

Jimmy Swaggart, age eleven, about 1946.

Minnie Bell Swaggart and son, Jimmy, about 1937.

109

W.L. Swaggart, Jimmy and Minnie Bell, about 1936.

Nannie, Uncle John, Aunt Rene on a Sunday when Nannie was speaking.

110

Jimmy Swaggart taping a television program.

Cousins—David Beatty, Jerry Lee Lewis and Jimmy Swaggart—in 1976 at LSU, Baton Rouge, Louisiana, where Jerry Lee was giving a show.

Hear . . .

Evangelist
JIMMY SWAGGART

January 2 thru 16 • 7:30 p.m.

★ **Every Night Except Saturday** ★

LINDALE ASSEMBLY OF GOD

JAMES McKEEHAN, Pastor

500 Caplin at Helmers • Northside Houston

JIMMY SWAGGART
Evangelist

A card advertising a Jimmy Swaggart meeting in Houston, Texas.

Jimmy Swaggart during his T.V. program with The Rambos.

112

A crowd responds to evangelist Jimmy Swaggart's invitation on behalf of the Lord Jesus.

113

Jimmy Swaggart Evangelistic Association offices in Baton Rouge.

114

Donnie and Debbie Swaggart.

9
A NEW
OLDSMOBILE 88

By the summer of 1958 Jerry Lee had become a national celebrity with his popularity surpassing even Elvis Presley's. During the eighteen months following the release of his first record, he had sold more than twenty-five million records. It was in the midst of all this heady success that a bombshell burst.

Jerry Lee had divorced his second wife, Jane Mitchum, and married his thirteen-year-old cousin, Myra Gale Brown, in December of 1957.

News of the marriage burst before the public while he was on a tour of England. As their pictures were splashed in newspapers around the world, the tour collapsed in the face of an angry outcry from the public.

Screaming headlines like "Jerry Lee Lewis Banned in England," "Rock Idol Marries 13-Year-Old Cousin," appeared on every newsstand.

I was in Spring Hill, Louisiana, preaching a revival, when Jerry Lee returned from England. Things were bad. Many of his shows in America had been canceled and some radio stations were even refusing to play his records. I decided to give him a call. If he ever needed a friend, it was now.

I dialed his telephone number and surprisingly he answered the phone. "Where are you, Jimmy?" he shouted enthusiastically.

I was stunned. He didn't sound like he needed cheering up to me. He sounded like the happy-go-lucky Jerry Lee I had always known. He hadn't changed. He was just as reckless as ever. He didn't care what anyone said about him. Why should he? He was already a millionaire.

"I'm in Spring Hill," I answered.

"I preached a revival up there once," he announced. "I'll be there tomorrow night."

"Come ahead," I replied knowing full well his appearance would disrupt the services.

That night I announced Jerry Lee would be

attending the services the following evening. The response was as I expected. People jammed into the tiny church building like sardines. Some couldn't find seats and had to stand in the front door or attempt to peer through the raised windows.

I don't think anybody heard a word I said that night. They were all looking at Jerry Lee and Myra whose recent photos in the papers made them seem even larger than life itself.

Afterwards we went out to a restaurant. Once again people jammed the place trying to get a picture or an autograph from Jerry Lee. Finally the owner ushered everybody out and locked the doors. Then it was his turn to go crazy. He couldn't get over the fact an internationally known celebrity like Jerry Lee Lewis was actually dining at his restaurant.

"I don't want you to pay for anything," the excited man repeated continually, "just let me say you came here to eat."

"Sure," Jerry Lee responded, "go to it." He was amused by all the clamor.

Looking at the menu, I forgot momentarily I was not paying for the meal. "I think I'll have a hamburger," I announced.

"No, Jim," Jerry Lee insisted, "get yourself a steak. Besides, the owner's paying for it."

In short order, Jerry Lee had ordered steaks for everybody and we were trying to cut through the tough pieces of meat.

Myra suddenly spoke up as we ate. "Jimmy," she said, "I told Jerry Lee he could buy you a new car and just take it off his taxes."

I almost swallowed my fork I was so surprised. For three months, I had been asking the Lord for a new car. "Not a Ford, Lord, but an Oldsmobile. And while you're at it, why don't you touch Jerry Lee and make him buy it for me."

People had laughed when I predicted Jerry Lee was going to give me a car. "His own sister wants one," somebody mentioned, "and he won't give her one." But I prayed believing—as Nannie had taught me.

"Yeah," Jerry Lee said, gesturing with his knife, "I've been thinking about that. It's a shame my cousin is driving around here to revivals in that rattletrap out there."

Everybody at the table laughed at Jerry Lee's description of my car.

"Can you be home Monday morning?" he asked. "Maybe we can get you a car then."

"I sure can," I answered. My heart was about to explode I was so overjoyed.

Monday morning we drove out to the Ford place in Ferriday. Jerry Lee fancied himself something of a horse trader and he immediately began haggling over the price of a car with a salesman. I stood back praying. I still didn't want a Ford. "Lord, you promised me the car I wanted," I reminded the Almighty, "and I don't want a Ford. I want an Oldsmobile."

The deal on the Ford got crossed up so we drove over to the Pontiac place and the identical scene was repeated. "Do you mind looking at an Oldsmobile?" I finally suggested to Jerry Lee.

"There's none here in town," he answered.

"There is over in Natchez," I prompted.

"Well, let's go over there," he agreed.

I was driving a green and white Dodge at the time and on our way to Natchez Jerry Lee began looking over the car. "You know, Jim," he said running his hand over the seat covers, "you've got a fairly decent looking car here."

His remark unnerved me. "Lord, tear this thing up or we'll never get a new car," I whispered under my breath.

Suddenly the engine began skipping and every time we took a sharp turn in the road the brakes scraped against the wheel drum producing a burnt rubber smell.

"Lord, help us," Jerry Lee said excitedly, "I hope we get to Natchez before this thing falls apart."

Thirty new Oldsmobiles were lined up in a row when we pulled onto the lot in Natchez. Jerry Lee and a salesman walked down the row of cars while I walked over and examined the one I had picked out.

"You can have the car you want but not the color

you want," God seemed to say to me. "You can have the tan and white car." No sooner had the Lord spoken, than Jerry Lee and the salesman stopped exactly behind that car. Within minutes the deal had been made and we were on our way back to Ferriday.

I called mama and daddy with the good news and they drove out to Jerry Lee's house in Ridgecrest. Mama put her arms around his neck and tried to thank him for his gift.

"Aunt Bell," he said in a soft voice, "God called me to preach and I'm a long way from it. I'm not living like I should and this won't take the place of it, but maybe God will have mercy on me."

We were very grateful for the car. Ultimately I would drive it over a hundred thousand miles in revivals all over the country with only minimal repairs. It was a real gift from heaven.

In the late 1950s I wanted to get as many people into our meetings as possible so in many places I let it be known that I was Jerry Lee Lewis's preacher cousin. I would also have special nights in the meetings when I preached a youth message and talked about my experiences with Jerry Lee. On those nights, people would flock into the services. We had scores of people who came to hear about Jerry Lee and wound up accepting

Jesus Christ as their Saviour. That was the real purpose anyway.

Using Jerry Lee's name in my revival meetings proved successful in attracting people to the services. But it worked against me in other avenues, especially when I applied for ordination in the spring of 1959. I was refused.

Frances and I had been traveling in full-time evangelistic work for well over a year when my name was presented for ordination. It came at a district council meeting of the Assemblies of God in Lake Charles, Louisiana.

Each of the candidates for ordination was being individually called into a room to be questioned by a committee of preachers. The district superintendent was polite but firm. "We can't ordain you," he said.

"But I don't understand," I replied. "Why? You're ordaining men who're not even full-time in the ministry. My wife and I have proven ourselves. Our record speaks for itself."

"Well, Jimmy," the superintendent intoned, "we are aware that you've been on the field for a year but we think there's more to ordination than time. There are other factors."

There was something about the tone of the man's voice that seemed to suggest I was not responsible enough to be ordained. Yet the committee's answer had been so vague and evasive I could read almost anything into it, but nothing concrete.

"Well gentlemen," I said openly, "I'll do exactly what you say. If I'm doing something I shouldn't, please say so. If there's something I should do, please say so. You're my elders and my brothers in the Lord. I'll do whatever you say."

James Allen, one of the preachers on the committee, interrupted me. "I can't see how anyone could object to a spirit like this. This man is showing a beautiful spirit and I, for one, would like to go ahead and resolve the situation now."

The district superintendent overruled Brother Allen. "I'm sorry," he said firmly, "we've already voted not to ordain Jimmy Swaggart at this time. He'll have to request ordination at next year's meeting."

But nobody would tell me exactly why. I walked out of the meeting totally crushed. We had already had such a struggle getting meetings. Now with this hanging over our heads the situation seemed almost hopeless.

There had always been a lot of rumors circulated about me. Being Jerry Lee's cousin, I guess that was normal. But I knew that being refused for ordination all boiled down to being his cousin. That bothered a lot of people. Others didn't like my piano playing and singing. They thought it wasn't churchy sounding enough. There seemed to be more rhythm in it than they thought the four walls of the church could stand.

Daddy and mama were both deeply hurt when I

told them about being refused. I was the only preacher denied ordination that day. Frances and I drove back to Wisner with a gloomy cloud hanging over our heads. Any time I got discouraged Frances always managed to put strength and encouragement back into me. But this time both of us felt like we had been kicked in the stomach by an Arkansas mule.

Back home, I walked into our bedroom and closed the door. I knew the devil could use this situation to make me bitter. "Lord," I said getting down on my knees beside the bed, "I'm going to stay in this room until there is no rancor or bitterness in my heart. I'm going to stay here until I can love these men who oppose me, just like I love my best friend." I stayed there for the rest of the afternoon and into the evening. Finally the joy began to flow again and I came up shouting and praising the Lord—even for this.

The next morning at the breakfast table, I was sipping an early morning cup of hot chocolate before Frances and Donnie awoke. I noticed Frances had not turned the little daily Scripture cards she kept on the table, so I did it for her. The blue card read Isaiah 54:17. I glanced at it. "No weapon that is formed against thee shall prosper."

Once again the presence of God filled my heart. No matter what happened with this ordination problem, the Lord would fight my battles. His strength would blunt every potential foe. I could count on it.

During the months that followed, I continued preaching as God opened the doors of churches throughout Louisiana and Arkansas. Then, the Lord gave us an exceptional revival with Pastor Robert Rogers in Atmore, Alabama. Brother Rogers was not one who rejected my music. He recognized the music ministered to people. He knew that such music was a gift of God. As he began telling other pastors about me, I began to get more calls for revivals than I could schedule.

Crisscrossing the southeastern states, we sensed the Lord was bringing revival. I never went the route some evangelists take—big cars, flashy clothes. I wanted a genuine, deep moving of the Holy Spirit, with bodies healed, people saved and lives changed—not just a lot of frothy excitement. Even as God moved in our services, I wanted more.

In January, 1960, I attended a preacher's seminar in Monroe, Louisiana. I was still plagued by criticism of my ministry, and worried by thoughts of not being able to get a decent start in my home area. "If you can't make it here, you'll never make it anywhere," I told myself.

A.N. Trotter, a man who had given many years

to serve as a missionary in Africa, spoke on the subject, "The Miracle River and the Holy Ghost." Using Ezekiel 47 as his text, Brother Trotter compared Ezekiel's river with the Holy Spirit. "Everything touched by the river shall live," he said.

"You must have the life of the Holy Spirit in you to live," he preached. "You find a church where the Holy Spirit is not moving and it's dead. You find an individual who is stale and stagnant and I'll show you a person who isn't moving in the Holy Spirit."

He preached for almost an hour, his every word bringing life to the congregation. Everyone sensed the presence of God.

Parts of Brother Trotter's message sounded like the story of my own ministry. As a young preacher, his own brethren had fought him. Instead of helping, they did everything to discourage him. He had come to the end of the road financially several times. But at a particular camp meeting, an elder preacher came and laid hands on him. The prayers of that preacher seemed to be the turning point of his ministry.

At the close of his message the entire congregation of three hundred preachers moved en masse to the altars. Men were sobbing before God. I was on my knees among them, praying.

"Lord, what I've heard this man say has strengthened me. I know it's asking a lot, but would you have him come over and lay his hands on me?"

At that moment Brother Trotter, who had never met me, walked down off the platform and made his way through the praying, weeping preachers. He walked past me, then came back. Stopping directly behind me, he laid his hands on my shoulders and began praying. I could almost hear the voice of the Lord whispering, "I'm with you and I love you. My Spirit is with you. The anointing this man has spoken of is going to be in your life and ministry, too."

That night I raced home and woke Frances to tell her all about the service. Brother Trotter's prayer had been like the hand of God on my shoulders. Facing opposition from good people who believed they were right, I had slipped into a depressed state of mind. Had they told me specifically why they refused to ordain me I could have corrected it. But since they only dealt with generalities I had allowed myself to believe I was inferior. That condition was now changing. I knew God was leading me.

Riding in a car following a Sunday morning service, Pastor L.O. Waldon reminded me of God's ability in leading His people. Brother Waldon knew about the problems I had faced over ordination. "The Word says if you commit your way unto God . . . He'll bring it to pass," he said.

As he spoke, I felt lifted and inspired.

He continued. "No matter who you are . . . if you obey the Word, it can happen. God gives direction to those who commit their lives to Him."

Not only did the Lord use people like A.N. Trotter and L.O. Waldon to encourage me but He also greatly used my mother. In my first few years of preaching, she was a source of constant inspiration and strength. People loved her for the soft, tender way she dealt with them. She seemed to have a personal touch with folks that overcame any problem or barrier. Mama used that same touch on me.

It wasn't what she said, but the way she said it which helped. "God has called you since you were a child," she often reminded me. "He has much better things in store for you than this. Now you give this ministry all the strength and energy you have."

It was the same strength and energy she imparted to daddy who had become pastor at Calvary Assembly in Baton Rouge. Any time he was preaching, she would be right there with her amen, encouraging him with all her heart. She had finally quit playing the guitar because of my kidding "it wasn't ladylike." But she sang frequently at meetings while I played the piano.

In the spring Frances and I left for another revival in Atmore, Alabama. I was backing the car out of the driveway when mama came out of the house toward us.

"I just wanted to kiss everybody good-bye one more time," she said wistfully. She walked around the car, hugged and kissed Donnie and Frances, then walked back to my side.

"Son, I'll be waiting," she said, looking forward to seeing me at my ordination service which meant so much to both of us. We had just learned of my acceptance for ordination.

I grinned. "Mama, I'll see you."

Things seemed strange that week in Atmore, almost unearthly. During the days I would go up to the church and pray for long hours. The Holy Spirit seemed so near. It was as though God was preparing me for something.

I got a letter from mama, explaining she was having some minor surgery. That's all I knew until Aunt Stella called saying mama had suffered a heart attack on the operating table and was unconscious.

Immediately, we packed up the car and headed for home. Thirty miles outside of Atmore, Frances noticed how nervous and upset I was. "Let's pull over in Bay Minette," she suggested. "You can call the hospital. Perhaps then it'll be easier for you to drive."

In Bay Minette I pulled into a service station operated by Fred Davidson, a man who had been saved in a previous revival meeting in Atmore. He pointed me to a wall telephone when I told him I needed to make a call.

Aunt Stella answered the phone. "This is Jimmy," I said. "How is mama doing?"

There was a long silence on the other end. "Aunt Stella, are you still there?" I asked nervously. "Can you hear me? How's mama doing?"

Then I heard Aunt Stella weeping. "Son, your mama's gone."

I don't remember saying good-bye to Aunt Stella. I just hung up and stood with hot tears stinging my eyes, staring vacantly at the gritty, concrete service bay.

"What's the matter?" Fred asked, placing his hands on my shoulders.

I looked into his lined face, tanned by many hours of pumping gas in the bright sun. "My mother just died," I answered softly.

He started crying too. "You know, I met her last year in Atmore. She and your dad. Is there anything I can do?"

I shook my head. "No, nothing."

As we drove, Frances and I recalled our last conversation with mama. She had said, "I'll be waiting," and now I knew she would—in heaven. I had said, "I'll see you," and that's one promise I knew I would keep.

The grief I felt was worse than any physical pain. After seeing daddy, I almost wished he could have died with her. He was like a man who had lost part of his body. He suffered horribly. And yet, there was nothing I could do to ease it.

All I could do was cry with him.

Jerry Lee, Mickey, David, Cecil and several other cousins served as pallbearers. David closed down a revival to come. Jerry Lee canceled several shows and was later sued because of it. But he loved mama and came to pay his last respects.

My sister Jeanette had married and had a home of her own, so Frances and I moved to Baton Rouge to be with daddy.

After a few days daddy remarked, "I want you to stay and help me pastor the church." It sounded good. The evangelistic work had been hard, staying in hotels, motels and many church basements. The work had been rewarding, but it had also been very difficult.

I agreed and entered the work full time, preaching almost every service since daddy hadn't been able to bounce back following mama's death. But as each day went by, I had a growing feeling of restlessness. This wasn't what I had been called to do. I was willing to help daddy for a while. But I knew I was not to stay permanently. Soon daddy also realized it. Six weeks after we moved to Baton Rouge we went back on the road. This time for good.

Back during my days as a swamper I developed

an awful headache one day while oiling the dragline. It was so bad I finally had to see a doctor. He examined me and sent me to a specialist who diagnosed my condition as an allergy. He was unable to help me so I tried another doctor. "This is the worst I've seen," the new doctor agreed. "I've never seen an allergy like this."

My head often seemed tight, my sinuses clogged and at times I had difficulty breathing. "What if I moved to Arizona or Florida?" I asked the doctor. "Would that help?"

"I don't care where you go," he answered shaking his head, "you're going to have the same problem. You are allergic to everything we've tested . . . pollen, dust, mold, mildew, animal hair. The only way to escape these things is to move into a vacuum."

And then he added the clincher. "You're going to have to learn to live with this thing," he said. "Just make your mind up to that."

I knew that wasn't the answer—especially for a Bible-believing child of God. But the next four years the allergy almost drove me crazy.

Sometimes I could hardly preach. It affected my delivery. Singing or talking with my nose clogged was impossible. Everywhere I went I carried a bottle of medicine, just in case. Sometimes I would break down and see a doctor. The only treatment was to put sticks up my nose in an attempt to open my sinus passages.

Every night right before I preached, I would step back in a side room and put drops in my nose or take a pill. I tried to believe God for my healing but nothing happened. At times I threw the medicine away as an act of faith but an hour later I would have to go back looking for it when the symptoms reappeared.

Finally one night in Chicago, I could go no further. It was icy cold. Snow was on the ground. We were lodged in a cold, drafty house while I was preaching a revival. Half the time was spent huddled up in blankets trying to keep warm. Following the service that night, I was ready to quit.

As usual, Frances was there to encourage me. "We're going to beat this thing," she said positively. "This is just another trick of the devil. He's just trying to stop us. If we can hold on long enough, I believe God will show us the way."

I really wasn't convinced. I had prayed for years seemingly without any results. We finished the meeting in Chicago and drove cross-country to Los Angeles for another revival. Instead of responding to the bright California sunshine, my allergy grew worse. My eyes ran continually. My nose was clogged and my head felt like it was encased in metal wire.

I went into a Sunday school room to pray before the service. "Lord," I said angrily, "I've made up my mind. I've taken my last pill. They tell me I have to learn to live with this thing. I'm not going to do it anymore. I may die, but I'm not taking the medicine anymore. You can either heal me or you're going to lose one evangelist. This is it!"

The power of God was stronger that night in the meeting than at any time I could remember. Many were saved and filled with the Holy Spirit. But my personal struggle went on. At nights I walked the floor gasping for air. Yet I refused to take the medicine. Instead I began to confess my healing even though there was no evidence for it. I kept repeating, "God has healed me, God has healed me." Many nights it took all the strength I had to confess those four words.

The battle continued for a full week. The enemy kept screaming in my ear as the symptoms grew worse. "You're out of your mind . . . just take a pill. You can get some relief. You can get some sleep."

But I held out. I refused to take the medicine and I kept confessing my healing. I didn't know much about healing, but I believed in it because God's Word declared its reality. I had prayed for others and many of them had been healed. It wasn't me. It was the Word of God taking effect.

The meeting closed and I still wasn't healed. Actually I was worse. We drove on to our next location in Stockton. I pulled the car up in front of Pastor Alfred Trotter's (A.N. Trotter's son) house while Frances went inside with Donnie. Pastor

Trotter came out to talk to me when suddenly the presence of the Lord drenched my body. Tears began sliding down my face.

"I feel it too," he said taking a deep breath, "but what is it?"

It felt like two fingers had just run the distance up my nostrils. I could breathe. "God just healed me," I cried amid the tears.

The Word of God had prevailed.

10
GOD KEEPS
A PROMISE

On several occasions Jerry Lee contacted me, urging me to record an album. He wanted me to record it at the Sun Record facilities in Memphis. Something about Sun bothered me, though. I didn't feel comfortable about Jerry Lee's suggestion.

Mickey hadn't made it with Dot Records the way he dreamed. He was now living in Houston where He kept trying to hit the big time. It was Mickey who told me about a small recording studio in

Houston.

"I can get the musicians and even arrange the session if you want to do it there," Mickey promised. Everything seemed right and I agreed to make the record in Houston.

My only experience with a record had come the year before when I cut a song called, "At the End of the Trail." It was done in Ferriday's only radio station with David Beatty serving as the producer. The musical background included my piano, a washtub bass and three girl singers known as The Harmonettes.

The record in Houston didn't turn out much better. In fact, it was so poor I went back to another studio in Houston and recut portions of it. I had borrowed money from the bank in Wisner for the record and I knew it had to be released.

The record, "Some Golden Daybreak," became an immediate favorite with people at our meetings. I knew we had picked out good songs: "Some Golden Daybreak," "What A Day That Will Be," "He Bought My Soul," "Stranger." Yet I felt as if God was trying to say something more through the comments of the people who were being blessed. It was as though he was telling me I was going to touch many people through records.

Frances insisted I send copies of the album to gospel radio stations. But I couldn't see that. "Why would anybody want my record?" I asked. "They've already got other gospel records by the

Statesmen and the Blackwood Brothers. Nobody wants my stuff."

She was adamant. "Well, I think the record is good and people would enjoy it."

Some nine months after mama's death, Frances and I were on our way to a meeting in Mobile, Alabama and we stopped off in Ferriday. I knew Nannie had been bothered by temporary paralysis in her left arm. I went specifically to ask her to see a doctor. A vibrant, alert woman, Nannie didn't act like an old woman. She hadn't visited a doctor or taken a drop of medicine in twelve years. She had always believed God for healing and up to now had always received. I knew I would have problems convincing her to go.

We had visited for a few hours when I brought the subject up. "Nannie, I want you to do something for me," I said.

"What is it?"

"You've been having these problems with paralysis," I said. "I'm concerned about it. I want you to have a physical."

"I'm not going to take any medicine," she snapped.

"They may not even give you any medicine," I answered. "But I'd just like to know what the problem is so I can pray more effectively. Won't you do it? Just for me?"

Nannie had been seated in her favorite cane bottom rocker with a cup of tea on her lap but she arose. Her gas heater clicked several times. The fall wind blew against the window screens as I stood waiting. Nannie seemed to be studying my question. "I'll do it for you," she said after a long pause, "but I wouldn't do it for anybody else."

We started out to the car. "Go back and put your arms around your grandmother," the Lord seemed to say. "You will not see her again here."

I began to cry. Walking back into her living room, I put my arms around Nannie and gently kissed her on the cheek.

The day of Nannie's appointment with the doctor, she awoke early with her left arm partially paralyzed. But to keep her promise to me, she forced herself to go to the doctor's office. While sitting in the waiting room with her brother John, she laid her head lightly on his shoulder. Uncle John didn't think anything about it. He knew she was tired.

When a nurse came to get Nannie for her appointment, she was still sitting with her head on Uncle John's shoulder. But she had already slipped away to be with Jesus.

The little Assembly of God church in Ferriday was filled and overflowing with people on the day of Nannie's funeral. But it wasn't like a funeral at all. It was more of a camp meeting. People sang and openly praised God. It was a time of joyful revival—just the way Nannie would have wanted it.

People walked away knowing they had been part of something special. The power of God had been so strong. Leo Young, the local mortician, approached me after the service. "Jimmy," he said with a puzzled look on his face, "I've been involved in many funerals. But I've never seen anything like this. People usually cry, but all these people were filled with joy. What was going on? What did I feel?"

I smiled at Leo. "You felt the power of God," I answered. "And you saw its effect on these people."

The loss of mama and Nannie in the same year grieved me deeply. Yet I was determined to make them a part of my ministry as long as I preached the gospel. They had meant so much to me, and I knew others would be blessed by the stories of their lives.

Not long after Nannie's death, I returned to Ferriday and visited Aunt Rene. She and Nannie had been extremely close, participating in daddy's meetings and even holding services of their own. In their fifties, they had even gone into an isolated area, erected a tent and held meetings.

"Jimmy," Aunt Rene said with tears in her eyes, "your Nannie prayed for you every day of her life and now she's gone. But I just want you to know I'm going to take up where she left off."

Tears filled up my own eyes as Aunt Rene spoke of her beloved sister. "I can't actually take her place," she said softly. "Nobody can do that. And I can't really pray as long as she did. But every day I'm alive I'm going to call your name in prayer before God."

I was so grateful for Aunt Rene's prayers. Many times I could feel them as Frances and I continued traveling the highways and backroads, from church to church and meeting to meeting. It seemed as if we were constantly packing, loading up, moving to a new location and then unloading, unpacking and getting reacquainted with the people.

What looked like an ill-fated teenage marriage years before in Wisner had become the greatest single gift to my ministry. In every situation, Frances seemed to supernaturally possess the wisdom and tact for handling it.

When things went poorly or I didn't feel the presence of God in the services, she was there to encourage me. Besides handling our clothing and personal items, she taught Donnie with the Calvert school method during his first four grades of grammar school. Even now I often wonder how she bore the load, but she never once complained or said she wished we were doing anything other than evangelistic work.

My first record, which I felt was poorly done, continued selling briskly in our meetings. At the same time Jerry Lee persisted in urging me to record an album at Sun Records. "Let's do it right this time," he had suggested. "I'll get the musicians for you and I think I can even get Sam Phillips to give you the studio time. The whole thing won't cost you a dime."

At that price, I could hardly refuse Jerry Lee's offer. "Okay," I agreed.

It wasn't that easy to do the record after we got to Memphis though. I wasn't a member of the musician's union and we suddenly found out that Sun was a union studio. I volunteered to join the union but it was impossible to get me in before the scheduled time for the recording. The whole situation looked permanently snarled. I didn't know what to do.

Jerry Lee and I were at his Memphis house trying to get the situation resolved. We telephoned other recording studios to see if we could get the record done elsewhere. We even tried appealing to the musician's union, all to no avail.

Jerry Lee always seemed to have a group of people hanging around him. They went on his tours, hung out at the studios, stayed around his house. Wherever he went, they went too.

During this time, a seedy-looking man with a permanent five o'clock shadow on his face and who was never without sunglasses was a house guest. He watched our frantic efforts and finally asked, "What are y'all doing?"

"We're trying to get a record cut for my cousin," Jerry Lee answered. "But we can't get the studio because the union has threatened to shut us down."

"The what?" the guy asked taking off his sunglasses for the first time.

"We've got to cut this record today because my cousin's leaving tomorrow and we can't get him in a union that quick," Jerry Lee explained.

It never occurred to us the man had any union connections. "Give me that phone and step out of the room for a minute," he suggested. "Let me see what I can get worked out."

In a few minutes he called Jerry Lee back into the room. "What is it?" I asked impatiently when Jerry Lee came walking out wrapped in a wide grin.

"We've got the studio and the musicians," he announced happily. "The union has even agreed to help us with additional sessions if we need it."

I was naturally overwhelmed when I entered the studio. This was the place that had produced the greatest hit records in the world during the late 1950s. The building itself seemed filled with power.

Scotty Moore, who had worked with Elvis Presley, engineered the session at no cost. He was in the control booth getting the sound board lined up and balanced. I was so scared my hands were trembling as I sat down at the big Steinway grand piano.

The musicians were tuning their instruments and giving microphone readings to the control booth. I knew the only way to make it through the session was to seek God's help. I bowed my head and began praying.

"Lord, I'm not here now at somebody's invitation. I'm here with no strings attached. I'm all yours and I'm asking you to help me with this recording. I can't do it by myself. My total strength comes from you and I'm believing you now for your help and anointing."

Even as I prayed I could sense the surging power of the Holy Spirit within me and moving through the studio. The place was filled with stale cigarette smoke. I was one of the few Christians present. But a peace and calm settled over the place. It took six hours, but when I got up from the piano the album was complete.

"That's one of the best sessions I've ever been in," Scotty Moore said slapping me on the back after we finished.

Most of the technicians and musicians had already vacated the studio and I was waiting on Jerry Lee to take care of some last minute business. Once again I sensed the Spirit of God moving upon me. Oddly enough, it was the same feeling I had experienced four years before when Uncle Elmo had tried to get me to record for Sun.

"Son, do you remember when I told you to trust me?" the Lord seemed to say.

I vividly remembered the day I stood weeping in the Sunday school room of the little Assembly of God church in Ferriday and heard God speaking. The scene had been permanently etched on my mind.

"Look at this big facility," the Lord suggested. "Elvis Presley was once here but he's gone now. Johnny Cash is gone. Charlie Rich is gone. Jerry Lee is leaving. There's nothing really left but a shell."

Running them over in my mind, I remembered one-by-one each of these big time entertainers who had once recorded with the studio. Yet for one reason for another, they had left. Jerry Lee was even leaving for another company.

"You can see now," the Lord continued, "that I led you right. I allowed you to use these facilities because they are the very best. But you came here on my terms, not theirs. My way is the only way because it will never bring disappointment and heartache. It always brings victory, peace and joy."

Tears slipped down my cheeks as I stood in the studio. "I see, Lord," I answered. "I see."

Years before God had saved me from tragedy. I had not made the mistake millions of young people make in some futile attempt to boost their ego by jumping at any chance to succeed. I knew accepting the Lord's direction for my life—even though it didn't look right at first—had proven correct. God had completely vindicated Himself in the situation.

Sometime later I was holding a meeting in Pontiac, Michigan, when a woman approached me after the service. "I work for Floyd Miles," she explained politely. "He owns a record store and sponsors a program over radio station WMUZ in Detroit. I'd like to give him a copy of the record to play over the air. Perhaps it'll help you and your ministry."

"Sounds good to me," I responded.

Up to that time my two albums had received only a minimum of air play on stations that programmed gospel music. Of course, the only outlet we had for selling the records was our meetings. But a change was in the wind.

True to her word, the woman passed the record to Floyd Miles and he gave it to Chuck Cossin, one of America's best known gospel disc jockeys. Cossin examined the record's bland looking black and white cover critically. "This is a piece of junk," he said throwing it across the room. "I'm not going to play that trash. Whoever heard of Jimmy Swaggart, anyway?"

Miles, who had played the record, had been touched. A month later he came back to Cossin. "Why don't you play this Swaggart record?" he asked. "People are coming in the store asking for it all the time. I believe it has potential."

Cossin was still unmoved by Miles' request, but, sometime later, in need of a record to fill blank air time, he played the record, "God Took Away My Yesterdays." The radio station's switchboard lit up like a Christmas tree.

Cossin was surprised, but I was stunned. Suddenly we began getting orders for hundreds of records a week from the Detroit area. Frances and I were doing all the labeling and shipping ourselves, sometimes from our car trunk and other times from motel rooms on the road. I couldn't believe the orders which continued to roll in.

I had turned down offers to record with several companies. They wanted me to record, yet they seemed intent on controlling my style of singing and playing. "None of that hallelujah stuff or talking on the records," I had been told. "We don't want that." So, I never recorded with any of those companies. I couldn't obey the Lord and follow those orders.

I had nobody to distribute my records and that's the name of the game in selling records.

Then I began praying, asking the Lord to distribute the records. Soon people began walking into record stores asking for my records. Little by little stores began contacting me for records. Then distributors began calling.

As the record albums began to sell, they produced a side benefit. More people were attracted to the services. As more people came to the meetings, the length of the revivals grew longer. In the beginning I had been preaching one and two week revivals, now they began to stretch into four and six week meetings.

I had prayed and fasted for many hours, hoping to see my revivals stretch into longer and more sustained periods of time. I knew the Lord could give that kind of revival but I had lacked the faith to believe for it. Now it was happening.

Even though we had many nights of great victory, there were other times when the services seemed stymied. If God had not moved in a service, I took the blame. Many times I felt God was displeased with me, or I didn't measure up.

One day, thumbing through a book, I found these words: "God is more interested with the worker than he is with the work." The truth of those words touched my heart.

Somehow God was telling me that every

preacher has his own struggles. It might seem like some preachers never face uncertainty and doubt, but they do. The devil is opposed to every work done in Jesus' name. But above all, God was saying He was more interested in Jimmy Swaggart personally than He was in the work Jimmy Swaggart was doing.

Knowing God was interested in me didn't relieve the struggle, but it helped me cope with the situation. Then I held my first revival with Pastor Hansel Vibbert at Calvary Temple in Evansville, Indiana, and God began stirring my faith.

A tremendous musician and singer, Vibbert had gotten his start with Eddy Arnold back in the Tennessee hills before going into the ministry. His singing greatly blessed the people even though he was likely to quit singing and begin shouting before he finished. An outgoing, happy man, Vibbert gave me a boost when I needed it the most.

After two weeks at Brother Vibbert's church, he approached me one night. "I've had everything in this pulpit that can walk or crawl and talk about Jesus," he said with a wide grin, "but your ministry is the greatest thing I've ever had."

"Well, I appreciate that," I responded, "but I thought we should close the meeting out soon."

"Oh no, I wouldn't think of doing that," he smiled. "Your music and message are exactly what we need. I've heard this cold, formal church music so much it's killing me. You've got the life we need here. I want to go on several weeks more."

Brother Vibbert's talk encouraged me. It made me realize I had something to give the people, something to minister. My faith began to grow and as it did the meeting stretched into four weeks. During that time, almost a hundred people were saved, many were filled with the Holy Spirit and others healed by the power of God.

The next meeting was with Pastor Lloyd Shoemaker at the Edwards Street Assembly of God in Alton, Illinois. It lasted six weeks. Crowds filled the church until there was no room to seat the people. Chairs lined the aisles. People stood in the vestibule and on the church steps. Over a hundred people were filled with the Holy Spirit.

Pastor Shoemaker responded to our ministry the same way Hansel Vibbert had. He recognized the touch of God on my life and readily told the people so. "You know, Jimmy," he told me one day, "when I first started out, I had a great problem with confidence."

"Is that right?" I responded as if I'd never been acquainted with the problem.

"That's right," he said, "but one day I came across Hebrews 10:35 about not casting away your confidence for it has a great recompense of reward. I had thrown it away and yet I was surprised when I didn't get any results. They go hand in hand."

It was hard to believe the man I called Laughing Lloyd, because he was always smiling, was ever lacking in confidence. He appeared to be the epitome of success and polish.

The problem he had described had always been mine. It seemed as if I never quite measured up to what God wanted from me. I had been taught what not to believe in—smoking, dipping, chewing, cussing, drinking—all the don'ts and none of the do's. There wasn't a positive element to it, and practically no faith. In the process, I had been filled with such negativism that I lost my confidence. And without confidence it was impossible to get results.

Now my faith was beginning to rise. I could see it was all possible. Truly all things are possible to them that believe. That is what Jesus said. It was true, really true.

Through the results of the Evansville and Alton meetings and the increasing demand for my recordings, I began to see my destiny was in the hands of a miracle working God. He loved me and was, in fact, on my side. Now I was beginning to see it was possible to touch thousands of people with His salvation, healing and the Holy Spirit.

Only time would tell what God would begin doing next. I could hardly wait to see what He had planned.

11
JESUS
LOVES SINNERS

Frances, Donnie and I were traveling north for a revival in Ohio when we stopped off in Memphis for an overnight visit with Jerry Lee and Myra. In spite of all the difficulties he had encountered with the press over his marriage, Jerry Lee continued to make hit records.

After driving most of the day from Baton Rouge, the three of us arrived and found Jerry Lee's house full of people. His house had always been filled with people of varying sizes, shapes and pedigrees. This night was no different.

Frances bedded Donnie down for the night and walked into the den where most of the people were congregated. A tall, swarthy man dressed in a flashy azure blue suit and a hefty diamond on his pinky, seemed to be the object of everybody's attention. A Las Vegas club owner, he was regaling everybody with tales of the big name entertainers and Hollywood stars who gambled at his place. From the tone of the conversation, he was a trusted confidant of them all.

"Yeah," he revealed, "some of these cats think nothing of dropping several grand a night playing blackjack or roulette. It's peanuts to them . . . they're making so much dough. They don't miss it."

For thirty minutes the club owner rambled on about his friends in Vegas. Most of the talk was centered around money and its power to bring unlimited pleasure.

Sipping a glass of tea I sat on a couch within earshot of the club owner and his crowd and asked the Lord for an opportunity to witness to these people. I was certain that Frances and I were the only Christians present.

Right in the middle of one of the club owner's stories, his wife—a platinum blonde who looked much younger than her husband—interrupted. "You're Jerry Lee's cousin, Jimmy Swaggart,

154

aren't you?" she inquired looking directly at me.

"Yes," I smiled somewhat startled.

"Don't you play gospel music and make records?" she questioned.

"Yes, I do."

"Would you come in here where the piano is and play some gospel songs for us?" she asked.

Immediately everybody agreed, saying "Let's do it."

"Yeah, come on," Jerry Lee joined in motioning everyone toward the living room.

As they filed out of the room, I lingered back momentarily asking the Lord for help. "I don't care if they see any talent in me," I appealed to the Lord, "I just want the songs to touch them."

Jerry Lee's living room was an interior decorator's dream, complete with a miniature waterfall and a stream of water trickling through the room. His concert grand piano was white and tastefully blended with the snow white shag carpet and soft lavender draperies.

As the people gathered around, I sat down at the piano and began playing and singing, "What a Day that Will Be." Even as the words flowed out of my mouth, I could sense the presence of the Lord in the room. That heavenly nearness seemed to intensify as I began to sing another song, "I'll Never Be Lonely Again."

I looked up while singing and practically everybody in the room was sobbing. It was as if

155

every person there had lost a close loved one. Tears were rolling down Jerry Lee's face. The Las Vegas club owner wasn't crying but he was trembling all over. His face was chalky white.

Slowly the people drifted out of the room, one-by-one, weeping as they went. In a few moments only Frances and the club owner's wife remained with me in the room. The woman was slumped forward on the soft lavender sofa, her shoulders shaking and great, racking sobs coming from her body.

I reached over and put my hands on her shoulders. "You may not know what is happening," I said. "You may not understand it . . . but the Spirit of the Lord is dealing with you. Jesus Christ loves you and He wants you to give your heart to Him."

Her reaction startled me. "God . . . no," she exclaimed balling up her fist and pounding the couch, "Please stop. I can't take any more."

I thought I had offended her. "I'm sorry, I didn't mean to upset you," I said attempting to apologize.

"No . . . no, that didn't offend me," she cried with tears running dark from her mascara. "I have to tell somebody. My husband doesn't even know this. I'm sure you can tell he's much older than I. I married him for his money. This is my third marriage and even with all the money it's not working out. But what nobody in this room knows is I used to be saved and filled with the Holy Spirit."

My heart almost flipped over as she spoke. "When you started singing tonight," she continued, "it brought back all the memories to me. I could see the little church where I grew up. I could see the altar where I knelt and gave my heart to Jesus. I could even picture myself in the choir where I once sang."

"For God's sake girl, why don't you come back to the Lord Jesus?" I appealed. "He loves you and wants to take you back."

"I know I must," she admitted helplessly, "I realize that. But if I do, I'll lose everything. I can go into the most expensive stores in America now and buy anything I want. I rub shoulders with movie stars, entertainers, sports heroes . . . some of the biggest names in the world. If I come back to Jesus, I'll lose all of that."

I nodded my head. "Yes, you probably will," I agreed. "But you're going to lose it anyway. No one ever keeps anything the devil gives him. After a while, he reclaims it all—as well as your own soul. What Jesus gives is so much better. What you're living now is false. It's not real."

"I know it," she sighed, "I've become so disgusted with it all. Night after night, I scrub my body until it's red and raw because I feel so dirty with what I've been doing. I try to scrub away the filth but I just can't. Night after night, I cry myself

157

to sleep because of the loneliness and the emptiness."

"You're telling me the same thing I'm telling you," I pleaded, "and yet you won't come back to Jesus? Why?"

Tears ran fresh down her face. Her lips trembled. She dabbed her eyes with a twisted Kleenex. Without saying another word, she jumped up from the couch and ran from the room. I looked at Frances in amazement as tears filled her own eyes. We both knew the girl had made a fatal mistake resisting the outstretched arms of the Saviour.

Together we walked back to the doorway of the den where everyone had fled. They were all laughing and talking again. Somehow they had been able to shake off the convicting power of the Holy Spirit. Even the Las Vegas club owner had his plastic smile back in place.

"I can't go back in just yet," I explained to Frances. "You go ahead and I'll be back in a few minutes. I want to go outside and be alone."

I found a door that exited outside and I stepped through it. A full moon reflected off the water in Jerry Lee's piano-shaped swimming pool. On the far side of the pool was a bath house in the form of a musical note. I stood for a few moments gazing at the stars as the night air's cool touch bathed my face.

"Lord, you'd think just by looking at all the

glitter and glamour in that house everything is well with those people's lives," I said, "but once you get beneath the surface there's nothing but loneliness, disappointment and heartache."

Joy flooded my soul and I began crying. "Father, I just want you to know I'm glad I made that commitment to you in that little church in Ferriday, Louisiana. I'm glad that my fate is in your hands. I trust you to know what's right for me in all things."

The Lord responded to my renewed commitment of trust. Deep in my spirit I could hear Him say, "As you look at the heavens, I want you to know I formed the rivers and the streams. I carved the mountains. I made man out of the dust of the earth. I made all the flowers to bloom. And you are an heir to all my riches. It is all yours . . . if you will simply follow me where I lead."

Frances and I had nothing of the world's goods—at least not the kind back in Jerry Lee's house. Yet we had everything worthwhile. We had Jesus.

12
THE
CAMP MEETING
PREACHER

Donnie was in the fourth grade. Even though he was responding well to Frances' private teaching as we traveled, it was time to slow down—for his sake. It was time to enter him in public school. Since my revival meetings were averaging four to six weeks, he could spend at least that much time in one school. But once the revival ended, we would move to a new location—and Donnie would have to start all over again in a new school, with new teachers, and new friends.

Sometimes he would come home upset after being enrolled at a new school. "Daddy, they don't seem too friendly at this school," he would say seriously. "What can I do about it?"

It was a real problem for a nine-year-old boy and we discussed ways he could make friends with the other kids. Somehow he always managed to find a buddy. At times we even played games with Donnie, just to see how many friends he could make in school before we moved to a different town.

Sometimes in changing schools, there would be large gaps in what Donnie was studying. Teachers and principals told us it was impossible for a child with his schedule to learn anything properly, but Donnie's grades never reflected their predictions, except once in Alabama.

I was closing a month long revival that Friday night and Frances had driven to the elementary school to pick up Donnie. His report card showed failing grades in several subjects. Knowing there had to be some mistake, Frances took Donnie home and drove hurriedly back to the school.

"That's exactly what Donnie made," the matronly teacher replied when Frances walked in and asked about the failing grades.

"There must be some mistake," Frances asserted positively, "I have all of his papers. There's not a single failing grade on any of them.

In fact, they're all A's and B's. Is it possible Donnie hasn't shown me all of his papers. Do you have any?"

"No, that's it," the teacher snapped.

Frances noticed the woman had a strong, defensive attitude. She sensed there was more involved than Donnie's academics. "Well, I'd like to see your gradebook then," she suggested, "there must be some reason for Donnie's failing grades."

"No, I can't do that," the teacher answered nervously adjusting her glasses, "it's against school policy."

"It's either let me see the book or we're going to the principal's office," Frances said determinedly. "When Donnie was enrolled here, I explained to you and the principal how he has to transfer schools frequently because his father is in the ministry."

"Yes, I know about his father," the teacher responded with a touch of animosity.

"Oh, you mean you've heard of him?" Frances asked quickly.

"Oh, yes," the teacher answered disgustedly. "My sister's only daughter has been to that revival where your husband was and she's gotten real mixed up. She went to the altar and got what you people call saved. I don't approve of such things and her mother and I are going to do everything possible to stop this."

"Is this the reason you've given my son a failing grade?" Frances demanded angrily. "Because you don't like God?"

The woman's eyes grew red and then filled with tears. The room grew silent, then the teacher unlocked her desk and brought out the disputed grading book. Donnie's grades were all A's and B's. The teacher offered no more resistance and obligingly changed the grades.

But it was a hard life for the little fellow. He was attending six to ten different schools a year. Besides trying to make a home for us wherever we were, Frances spent many hours helping Donnie keep up his studies. The rest of the time was spent either on a church pew or in a car on the way to a meeting.

One afternoon during a revival meeting in Jackson, Alabama, I became so discouraged over the perplexing situation that I fled into the pastor's study to be alone and seek God. I had some decisions to make. Daddy was leaving the pastorate of Calvary Assembly in Baton Rouge and the job had been offered to me.

"Lord," I pleaded, "if you'll let me take a church, I can raise my son like other boys. The road is no place to raise a family and the work is wearing me thin also. I feel we need a change, God."

I stayed on in the study praying until the afternoon sun began going down and shadows crept through the windows. I was still lying on the carpeted floor seeking God when I began to hear his still, small voice.

"Son, if you want to take a church," the Lord said, "I'll bless it . . . but if you want my perfect will, you will continue as you are doing."

The Lord's words confirmed what I already knew deep in my heart. I broke and wept freely. In spite of the weariness of constant travel, in spite of the pressure to bring genuine revival in the meetings, in spite of the problems with Donnie's schooling, I had to continue on.

"Lord, all of my life I've wanted your will . . . your perfect will," I resolved. "I've never asked for the easy way. I promise I will do exactly as you want. I know this is your calling for me and I'll continue on."

As before, that simple commitment didn't end the problems. They were still as real as before. But I had a new resolve. I knew with God's help that I could overcome any situation, great or small.

There were other problems. Just getting from one town to another presented difficulties at times. We were on our way from Broken Arrow, Oklahoma to Columbus, Georgia to start another meeting. Memphis was about midway. We stopped, spent the night with Jerry Lee and

Myra, and were on our way.

From the moment I arose that morning God's presence had been very near. I thought it was strange. I knew in times past when His presence was near—as with mama's death—He was fortifying me for something.

Then God spoke to me as I drove. "The devil is going to attempt to kill you today." It was like somebody had slapped me in the face. I was stunned. "What do I do?" I thought.

We stopped for breakfast later but I couldn't get the food down. While Frances and Donnie finished, I excused myself and went to the car to pray. Down the road, God's words weighed heavily upon me. I didn't want to upset Frances, so I said nothing. Tears filled my eyes. I brushed them away so she couldn't see.

The car whizzed along. "What do I do?" I whispered to the Lord.

"Do what you preach," came the response.

Immediately I began to claim divine protection. I thought about Job and the hedge which was around him. I claimed that hedge. I knew God would protect us against satanic hurt or harm.

Three minutes later, I topped a hill doing about sixty-five miles an hour. Down in the valley ahead, I saw a car stopped in the road. I knew if I jammed on the brakes I would plow into the car. I looked in the passing lane but another car was approaching. I couldn't pass! I looked to the right but a state tractor was cutting grass. That was why the car had stopped.

As if supernaturally directed, I cut left across the highway slamming into a thirty foot high earthen embankment, wham! The U-haul trailer I was pulling flipped over. Articles flew around in the car. The car stopped. The dust settled. I remembered hitting the brake but nothing else.

People converged on us from every side. One man's face was white as he jerked my car door open. "When I saw you top that hill," the man said excitedly, "I just knew there were going to be a lot of people killed. Are you okay?"

I looked around at Donnie and Frances. They appeared shaken but unharmed. "Yes, we're okay," I replied.

"What'd you do?" the man asked.

"I don't know," I said shaking my head.

We got out of the car and I surveyed the damage. The trailer was lying on its side but had not come loose from the hitch. Several men helped me turn it back on its wheels. I unlatched the trailer door. Everything was exactly as we placed it. Clothes, suitcases, musical instruments, records—nothing was damaged. The impact's only damage was to a small rim around a headlight.

The Lord's presence was growing so strong I was about to shout. I could hardly stand there. I thanked everyone, backed the car up and drove away. Almost instantly I began speaking in tongues—praising God in a heavenly language. Frances joined in. "What a Saviour," we agreed.

While preaching at Lloyd Shoemaker's church in Illinois, I asked the Lord to allow me to preach some camp meetings. Although very few of the camps were held in Louisiana, I realized that the meetings were an important ministry within the Assemblies of God. The camp meetings were normally held during the summer months for a week or two when people had more free time. They served as a spiritual filling station.

Even though only veteran preachers were used in most of the camp meetings, during the mid-1960s I began receiving invitations to participate in various camps. I felt inadequate, sharing the platform with men like A.N. Trotter, but I sensed God had brought him back into my life to help season me for the days and years ahead.

I determined to make the most of our times together. Between meetings, we had many opportunities to pray together and talk privately. It was an enriching time for me as Brother Trotter shared from the depths of his heart. His constant theme was the anointing of the Holy Spirit.

"Jimmy," he frequently told me, "when you play that piano, play the Holy Ghost through it. When you stand behind that pulpit, preach the

Holy Ghost through it. When you get on your knees in prayer, pray in the Holy Ghost."

"You know, Brother Trotter," I responded, "for the last several years I've come to understand exactly what you've been talking about. We can always do whatever needs to be done if we have the anointing of the Holy Spirit abiding on us."

"That's right," he replied smiling broadly, "preachers especially shouldn't depend on talent, ability or anything else. We can use these things but we must never rely on them. The Holy Ghost is the only one we must rely on. He alone is the agent for getting the job done."

My meetings were consistently running four to six weeks now, something unheard of within the Assemblies of God. Thousands of people were being saved and filled with the Holy Spirit. Many times whole churches were completely revolutionized by the power of God.

As word of our successful meetings spread, I began to get invitations to speak at practically every camp meeting within the denomination. I was becoming known as a camp meeting preacher. Favoring an old-fashioned brand of the gospel—the kind I was raised on by daddy, mama and Nannie—I guess it was natural for me to get such a label.

Following a camp meeting one summer in Indiana, I returned to the motel to rest before beginning services the following Sunday in a local church. Thumbing through a newspaper I discovered Jerry Lee was in town for a concert. It had been months since I had talked with him and the only way I knew what he was doing was by reading occasional stories in the newspapers.

After several calls to other motels, I learned he was staying in the same Holiday Inn one floor directly below us. "Where are you?" he shouted into the receiver when I called.

"Right above you," I laughed.

"Well," he responded, "come on down here before I come up there."

Frances and I walked downstairs to visit with Jerry Lee and found his youngest sister Linda Gail there. An excellent singer in her own right, she had just begun traveling in Jerry Lee's shows. We were casually talking and laughing about old times in Ferriday when Jerry Lee spoke up. "Hey," he said with a look of satisfaction on his face, "I understand the record I helped you cut is doing real good. In fact I heard it on the radio the other day."

"Yeah, it is," I answered. "The Lord is really blessing the album . . . and I really appreciate your help with it. It probably couldn't have been done without you."

"Good," Jerry Lee nodded.

"Everywhere we go people are constantly telling us what encouragement the record brings," I continued, "you know, Jerry Lee, the world is full of broken and hurt people needing exactly the touch this record gives."

The room was getting quiet as I described the blessings God had brought through the record, "God Took Away My Yesterdays." When I glanced at him, I noticed Jerry Lee was crying. So was Linda Gail.

"Jerry Lee," I said softly, "I know how the devil lies to you. I know how he lies to everybody. He's the father of lies and there's absolutely no truth in him."

As I spoke Jerry Lee cradled his head in his hands and nervously stroked his wavy hair. "If you give your life to God, you think you'll have to give up everything and live on beans. You think you'll have to drive a rattletrap car and lose all your fame and fortune. And maybe, for a while, you will. But it you'll live for God, He'll restore you. He'll repay you."

"I know it," Jerry Lee agreed through the tears, "I know it."

Yet in spite of knowing it, Jerry Lee simply would not make a commitment to the Lord. He was bound by an unseen fear. A fear that I knew would one day consume his life unless he turned to God. He had bought the lie of the devil that serving God is a life of poverty and hardship.

Even though Jerry Lee didn't surrender himself that afternoon, I renewed my commitment to keep on praying for him and witnessing to him. Months before I had begun to wonder what was the use of praying for him any more. It seemed like every time I picked up the newspapers Jerry Lee was involved in some kind of trouble or scrape with the law. I knew that everybody who committed themselves to the rock-and-roll life style eventually lost their Christian testimony.

"Don't ever stop praying for him," the Lord told me that afternoon. "As long as there is breath, there is hope." I knew the Lord was right and I committed myself to a diligent life of prayer in Jerry Lee's behalf.

Jerry Lee wasn't the only person with battles. I had my own, too. The continuing problem of demon oppression seemed never far away. Years before when I was starting into the ministry I had received victory over oppression using the name of Jesus. But through the exhausting schedule of meetings, the continuous preaching night after night, my physical body had grown extremely tired. When it did, the devil began to take advantage of the situation by working on my nerves.

172

For months I found myself saying, "I'm so nervous. I'm so nervous." Before long, I was in the habit of continually repeating that phrase to Frances, "I'm so nervous."

There was no reason to be nervous. I was having excellent meetings, some of the best within the denomination. The crowds were good with sufficient offerings. But at night, I couldn't sleep. I would walk the floor half the night. The next day I would be even worse from lack of sleep. I was uptight. My stomach was in knots, but I couldn't put my finger on the problem.

Frances tried to encourage me as usual, but nothing changed the situation. I sought God without any apparent success.

We were staying in a small house behind a church in Amarillo, Texas, where I was conducting revival services. Day after day I paced the kitchen floor, mumbling, "I'm so nervous." Every time I repeated the phrase I got worse.

Then the voice of the Lord spoke deep within me. "Don't ever say that again!" The Lord's words were so strong I stopped dead in my tracks. "Don't ever say that again!" He repeated.

I knew the Lord was trying to tell me something and I had to get alone. I told Frances to go ahead with lunch and I beat a path to the church. Opening a side door I moved toward the altar. "Lord, I know you're trying to tell me something," I cried.

The Lord's explanation came instantly. "What you're saying is real, very real. But when you confess your problem rather than my victory, you're just digging your own grave."

"Well, what do I do then?" I pleaded.

"When you feel this thing coming on you again," He admonished, "instead of confessing 'I'm so nervous,' you start praising the Lord."

That sounded hard.

"It will be hard at first," He continued, "but don't admit to that thing. Don't say it with your mouth. Start praising me and you can have the same victory I have. But don't be snared by the words of your mouth."

Snared by the words of my mouth. I never realized something as small as saying "I'm so nervous" was creating all my trouble.

Gradually I learned to get victory in the situation. It was not easy. In fact, it was like chewing sawdust at first. My basic reaction was to admit failure, but I hung on and victory began coming.

As I studied the Bible, I found countless Scriptures that backed up what the Lord had told me. Proverbs 18:7 said, "A fool's mouth is his destruction, and his lips are the snare of his soul." Proverbs 18:21 repeated almost the same thing. "Death and life are in the power of the tongue."

Then I discovered Jesus' words when He addressed himself to the same subject. "For by thy words thou shalt be justified, and by thy words thou shalt be condemned," He had said in Matthew 12:37.

As I discovered this dynamic principle, I began to watch carefully what I said with my mouth. As I did the problem with nerves disappeared.

That same Amarillo meeting had stretched into four weeks, and God had given us a stirring revival, helped along by my personal victory over nerves. Near the end of the four weeks, a short, plump woman had begun trailing after me at the end of each night's service. "I'm so nervous, I can't sleep at night," she whined continually at my coat sleeve, "I'm under the care of three doctors."

Night after night, I attempted to soothe her. But one night, I had taken all I could stand.

"Shut up," I snapped, turning around to glare at her.

Her mouth flew wide open. Tears brimmed in her eyes. "Don't ever say that again," I said trying to soften my words, "every time you say you're nervous you dig your own grave."

She sobbed for a few moments as I continued talking. "Whenever you feel this thing coming on, just praise the Lord. Praise will whip the devil every time." I walked off, not really knowing what she would do with what I said.

The phone rang at five o'clock the next morning. I reached out mechanically. "Hello, this is Brother Swaggart," I mumbled sleepily.

"It works! It works!" came an excited voice over the phone. For a few moments I didn't know what to say. I didn't realize who it was until she identified herself.

"What you said last night hurt my feelings," she exclaimed, "but after I went home I realized what you were trying to do. Last night I went to bed praising the Lord. I woke up briefly but I started praising God again and went right back to sleep. I've had the best night's sleep I've had in months. I've been taking medicine to make me sleep and I didn't take a drop last night."

That little woman became a renewed child of God by refusing to give the devil a place in her conversation, and by learning to praise the Lord when adversity and problems descended. As this principle became more real to me, I began sharing it with other preachers and friends. I was shocked at their response.

"Aw, Jimmy," they frequently told me, "that's nothing but mind over matter. That's all it is."

"But it's right here in the Bible," I maintained firmly. "I know it's not something we've always taught. But when God's Word declares something like this—it's got to work."

As I grew to understand the importance of a positive confession in a Christian's life, I closely watched those people who didn't agree with it. Most of them lived a life of infrequent victory. Sadly many of these people were preachers who were leading congregations in defeat.

I saw that positive confession would succeed in evangelistic work, too. I had preached two weeks in a large southern city, and the meetings had never really become a revival. It was a humdrum affair in spite of all the prayer I was putting into the services.

Then I noticed the church's pastor was continually saying, "Well, it's just hard to get crowds here during the week." On the weekends, he had a different alibi. "You can't get good crowds on the weekend," he maintained. "People are so involved in other things."

I made up my mind I didn't want to hear that kind of talk any more. I told Frances so when we got back to the motel. "I'm confessing God is moving in a mighty way," I declared positively. Together we agreed in prayer, fasted and sought God for a deep and lasting revival. And it came!

The church filled up night after night. People sat in the aisles and stood in the lobby as God moved. Souls were saved. People were filled with the Holy Spirit. Ultimately the revival stretched into four weeks.

"I don't understand it," the pastor shared with me later. "This revival seemed to be going nowhere fast . . . but then all of a sudden, the church began to pack out and the Spirit of God moved powerfully."

"Preacher, I've learned something here," I

replied seriously. "I heard you say over and over it's not possible to get a crowd in here. For a while I accepted it. But finally, Frances and I began praying and confessing positively we were going to have a revival. That's clearly what happened."

I had seen countless churches, people and situations exactly like that, wrapped up in traditions, past experiences, meetings and formalities. The Spirit of God rarely moved in those churches and among those people. I was determined to break that yoke of bondage wherever I preached.

13
900 LETTERS
AND A MIRACLE

Whenever we were in the Memphis area, I tried to stop and visit Jerry Lee. True to Jerry Lee's down-home manners, he always offered the large, ranch style house as a resting spot even if he wasn't at home.

I had never really owned a house and that concerned me. Often bone weary, physically and mentally tired, I yearned for a place we could call our own.

These thoughts lingered in the back of my mind

as we stopped at Jerry Lee's house one afternoon. He was away at a concert and the house was quiet and still. Frances cooked supper that night, and while she was cleaning up I silently padded through the house without my shoes.

Jerry Lee had told me about a new leather recliner he had recently bought. It was covered in green leather and cost $300. I headed for his den and sure enough there sat the rich-looking chair. Gloomy thoughts seemed to fill my mind as I stood looking at that chair and running my hand over its finish.

"You don't have a home," the thoughts suggested. "Your home is a motel room or a back room at a preacher's house. Just look at Jerry Lee. He's got it all. If you had gone with his people years ago, you could have things like this."

My head grew dizzy. For a few moments I felt weaker than I had in a long time. My resolve seemed to falter. Once again the facts suggested I might be following the Lord, but it was a hard road.

Somehow the words of the Apostle Paul came to mind, and I found myself speaking them. "For I reckon that the sufferings of this present time are not worthy to be compared with the glory which shall be revealed in us" (Romans 8:18).

Even as I quoted those words the presence of the Lord was upon me, giving my heart peace and assurance where moments before I had been faltering. How tempting it was to look at Jerry Lee's material possessions and wonder, what if? What if I had gone that way? What if I had taken Sam Phillips up on his offer? What if I had gone out on the gospel quartet circuit?

But inside I knew God's way had been better. All of those thoughts were just flights of fancy designed to get my eyes off the plan of God for me. "Romans 8:18," I sighed, walking back into the kitchen to check on Frances, "that's the way for me."

I had been recording an album each year and now I had a total of five records to my credit. Each one sold better than the last and the crowds coming to our meetings indicated the recordings were being well received. We had been able to save up a little money—a few thousand dollars—and the Lord began to assure me he was going to give me a house.

In the fall of 1967, we decided it was time to build. We picked out a nice corner lot in an attractive subdivision of Baton Rouge. After getting everything settled on the lot, I applied for a building loan at a local bank. In spite of my frequent calls, four weeks passed and the loan still had not closed. The bank seemed to be dragging its heels needlessly.

Finally I began appealing to the Lord in prayer. "These people are supposed to give me the loan for the house and they're not coming across," I prayed.

The Lord's reply startled me. "Don't get the loan," he said. "You don't need it. Go ahead and build."

"But I only have a few thousand dollars," I informed Him.

"Start it," came the reply, "you don't need the money."

The Lord's words were firm and sure. I felt I had heard correctly. That afternoon I returned to the bank. "It'll probably be some time before we can close that loan," the loan officer informed me as I walked in.

"That's okay," I replied smiling. "I came to tell you I don't need the money."

"Oh, we can have it later today," he brightened, showing a complete change of heart.

"No," I answered feeling more confident, "I don't need it now."

We moved ahead to build the house, trusting in the Lord's personal word to me. Each time we came back to Baton Rouge from a meeting, the house had taken more shape. Even more important, each time we had a bill, the money was in the checking account to pay it. The house was being built debt free.

I still owed several thousand dollars on the

house when I began holding services at Brightmoor Tabernacle in Detroit, in January and February of 1968. The Lord performed miracle after miracle in that meeting. First, thousands of dollars worth of records were sold in the services—enough to completely pay off the house. Then Donnie received the Baptism with the Holy Spirit.

Radio played a vital role in that Detroit meeting which ultimately stretched into eight weeks. It was the longest revival I had ever preached up to that time. During the eight weeks, I frequently appeared on WMUZ with Chuck Cossin. At times, he would interview me and play songs from the record albums. On the next occasion, I would answer questions from the listening audience. Because of this exposure to a radio audience, more people came out to the meetings. And I began to hear questions like "Why don't you have a program?" "You're a natural for radio," others suggested.

Something about radio touched me in Detroit. I saw it as a great tool for reaching people with the gospel. The Detroit meetings proved that. At the same time, my records were being played with increasing frequency on many gospel stations. In some locations I had the number one gospel record.

In the fall of 1968, Donnie entered the ninth grade. More than ever before I felt that Frances needed to stay home with him. Most of my church conventions and camp meetings were within the Assemblies of God, with revivals booked a year or more in advance. I was actually thinking about cutting back on my schedule to be at home more often. I felt our ministry had grown to the point God wanted it to be.

The results of the Detroit meeting and the role radio had played there had lasting influence on me. That spring, the Spirit of God began dealing with me about a daily radio broadcast. Although I knew radio was a powerful medium for dispensing the gospel, there were things about it that bothered me.

I was deeply troubled by a few radio evangelists who specialized in selling so-called miracle billfolds, prayer cloths and anointing oil over the airwaves. I detested such trickery and refused to be identified with it.

But the fact some were abusing the medium did not seem a sufficient reason to keep me away. Almost every time I went to my knees in prayer, I came up thinking radio. Finally, the Lord broke through and I heard what He was saying.

"I want you on the radio because I want you to stop this other kind of programming where the Holy Spirit is being hawked like a piece of cheap goods," the Lord informed me. "The world thinks everybody who believes in the Baptism with the Holy Spirit is this way. I want to dispel that thinking."

184

I recognized the truth of what God was saying to me. I knew there was a need for good counter-programming by legitimate religious broadcasters.

Then, He spoke prophetically, "I am going to send a wave of the Holy Spirit like the world has never seen before. I am going to pour out my Spirit upon the world. If you will obey me, this radio program will be a useful instrument of service to the Kingdom of God."

One of the radio preachers I respected was David Nunn of Dallas. That fall I paid him a visit and he briefed me on the general kinds of equipment I needed. I ordered some equipment from a Houston electronics firm and got the services of Len Benson, a Baton Rouge engineer, who helped me set up a rather makeshift studio.

It was all a faith move since I had no clear direction.

Shortly afterwards I was preaching at the Assembly Tabernacle in Atlanta, one of the largest Pentecostal churches in Georgia. We had held many long-running revivals there with Pastor Jimmy Mayo. One night, Warren Roberts, a local disc jockey, approached me after the service. "Say, Brother Swaggart," he exclaimed, grabbing my hand and pumping it soundly, "I'd like to get your radio program on my station."

"Warren, I don't have a radio program," I responded wondering where he was getting all that enthusiasm.

"Well, I heard you were going on radio," he said positively. "I think you ought to go on in Atlanta. You remember the success we've had every time you've been on the air with me."

"Your radio station has been a big help to us," I agreed, "but my program is just in the planning stages now. I'm not quite sure what we're going to do with it."

Ultimately Warren talked me into placing my radio program with his station in Atlanta. I signed a contract and returned to Baton Rouge to get my act together. I needed a name for the program plus some idea for a format.

"Well, you're preaching more camp meetings than anybody else and you've been called a camp meeting preacher," Frances said as we sat at the kitchen table enjoying cookies and iced tea.

"That's true," I agreed munching on a cookie. "What's the point?"

"Why don't you call it the Camp Meeting program?" she asked.

"I like the camp meeting part," I answered, "but it seems to lack something."

She thought for a few moments. "How about adding the word *hour*?"

"Well, it's not an hour but that has possibilities," I replied reflecting on the name. "The Camp Meeting Hour. That has a real down home touch. It really does."

Now that I had a name for the program, I began working on the format. I had just recorded "Someone To Care," and I decided to use it as my theme song. I decided to play a song off one of my albums, preach a short message and then close out the fifteen minutes with prayer.

Beginning January 1, 1969, "The Camp Meeting Hour" went on single radio stations in Atlanta, Houston and Minneapolis-St. Paul. For six months I made the tapes and shipped them to the stations. All of the money from my meetings was being poured into the radio effort, but the response was poor, very poor. In fact, the response was practically zero.

I had been in a revival meeting in Illinois and described the situation to the pastor. "Jimmy," he suggested, "you're going at it wrong. You've got to get up, beg for money and use whatever gimmicks you can. That's the only way you can survive financially."

"Well, I'm not going to do that," I replied. "I'll starve before I use gimmicks and tricks. If God raised the program up, I'm expecting Him to support it."

Back in Baton Rouge, I told Frances what that preacher had suggested. "Well, don't let that bother you," she answered trying to encourage me as usual, "God has a better plan."

"It's not bothering me," I asserted, "but I have decided to cancel the programs if we don't get any better response. I'll give it a few more weeks, but we can't continue the way we're going."

In spite of all the facts to the contrary, she answered me firmly. "God told us to go on radio," she reminded me. "Why, I don't know . . . but if we have to sell the furniture in the house, we'll do it to stay on radio."

I knew she was right. God had spoken to her regarding the radio ministry about the same time He had spoken to me. Even so, wavering, I continued with my plans to cancel the program.

The next week I began services in Louisville, Kentucky with Pastor Waymond Rodgers. Frances stayed home with Donnie. Somehow I knew it was a mistake to cancel the program, but I didn't know what else to do. Each night, following the services, I returned to the motel, walked the floors and prayed.

The sun rose several mornings to find me in that motel room still wide awake, eyes wet with tears. The Lord was dealing severely with me. "You're not right, you're not right," He seemed to say. But I didn't know what else to do. When nothing happened to ease the financial pressure, I wrote letters canceling the program on all three stations.

Unknown to me, two of the station managers called Frances immediately upon receiving the letters. Both of them said essentially the same thing. "We'll lower the rates on the program to a giveaway basis, but please don't cancel the program. It's too beneficial to the people and the station."

The third person, Warren Roberts, didn't even call. He simply preempted the radio broadcast and went on the air himself, telling the listening audience Jimmy Swaggart was canceling the program because of a lack of response.

"Folks, I don't feel the program ought to be canceled," he insisted, "and even if Brother Swaggart wants to cancel I'll play the same tapes over and over until they wear out. If you want the program to stay on, I want you to write him."

Three days later, Frances found a mailbag the postman had left on our front porch. She brought it into the house and with the help of a girl we had previously hired to type a few letters, they opened the pouch. It contained nine hundred letters and about three thousand dollars in donations for the radio program.

That afternoon, I called home to check on my family.

"I've got something to tell you," Frances announced cheerfully.

"What's that?" I asked, curious about her cheerfulness.

"Well, over nine hundred letters and something like three thousand dollars came in the mail today for the program," she cried joyfully.

I was stunned by the news. That was the last thing in the world I thought she might tell me. I broke down and bawled over the phone. "Oh, that's God," I sobbed, "that's God."

"There's no doubt about it," Frances replied, "God wanted us on radio and He performed a miracle to prove it."

At that moment I made up my mind to stay on radio. I began making plans to succeed, instead of fail. That miracle turned me around and changed my attitude in the process. I was there to sink or swim with the radio program. I realized, as never before, the formula for success was simply to follow God's direction.

That same summer, I went to a large camp meeting in Ohio. While the services were underway one night, the weather turned stormy. It thundered and lightning flashed as I preached and I began praying earnestly that we might finish the service as the lights flickered on and off.

After the service, Frances and I returned to our

small cabin on the campgrounds. Sometime around two o'clock in the morning, I was aroused by the sound of something striking the side of the cabin with a thump. I lay awake for a while listening to the sound of the pounding summer rain, yet, over that, I kept hearing the thumping noise. Finally, I got out of bed to investigate.

I was concerned about our little travel trailer which contained boxes of my albums plus equipment and clothing. It had been parked in front of the cabin, but when I looked out the window it was gone. Instead several feet of water were slapping against the sides of the small wooden cabin. The sudden, torrential downpour had created a flash flood.

My first thought was to get out of the cabin as quickly as possible. "Frances," I shouted, "get up. There's water all around the cabin. We're gonna have to leave."

The water was waist deep and swift, but we managed to struggle to the car holding hands. Surprisingly the engine started but the water was pushing with so much force the car wouldn't budge. Finally we got out and waded back into the cabin. The wind was howling, and the cabin shaking.

With Frances' help, I began piling our clothes and other things on shelves in case the water rose further. I threw a box containing invoices for album sales (representing hundreds of dollars owed to us) and other correspondence on the bed. We hurriedly struggled out the back door where the current was less rapid, to safety.

The next morning as I sat in my disheveled clothes with waterlogged shoes, I began thinking about all the invoices and important papers I had left at the cabin. "I need those papers," I finally suggested to Frances. "If I don't have them, we're going to lose quite a bit of money that we need for radio time."

She was not too keen on the idea of me going back to the cabin. But a man who had attended many of my services in Beckley, West Virginia volunteered to go back with me. The cabin was located near a small stream which had suddenly swollen to the size of a river from the downpour. The water was so swift and deep a Volkswagen had actually floated by us the night before.

Unknown to us, the rushing water had washed deep potholes around the cabin. As we inched around the sides of the cabin holding onto each other, I suddenly stepped into a hole.

I quickly got my head back above the water but the strong current was pulling me underneath the cabin. I kept trying to hold onto the cabin's siding with the current tugging at me fiercely and my companion holding to my waist.

"If you fall into this hole, we'll both drown," I shouted at him but he continued clinging to me.

"Oh, God help us," he screamed above the sound of the rushing water.

It seemed as if we struggled for half an hour against the raging current of water even though I know it must have been just a few minutes.

Somehow we got our footing and stumbled back to dry ground. Finally we were able to get a boat and navigate the waters back to the cabin. Inside we found the box still on the mattress which was now floating in five feet of water. All of the papers were dry and safe. All of the equipment in my trailer and our clothes had been ruined. My car was a total loss. But all of that was replaceable.

What I could not have replaced was my life and my wife's life. I sensed in my heart it was a crucial time in my ministry. The devil had tried to take our lives and I realized the struggles would become more intense as I moved forward with God. For years to come, I would dream about struggling against that current and almost drowning. Each time I dreamed about it I woke up in a cold sweat.

Two weeks later I was preaching at a large Assembly of God church in Fort Worth where my friend, Ken George, pastored. Afterwards an elderly woman walked up to me and tapped me on the shoulder. "Brother Swaggart, can I talk to you?" she asked.

"Sure," I responded.

"Did you have some trouble on the early morning of July 4th?" she questioned wiping a sprig of gray hair from her eyes.

Recognizing it was the date and the time I almost drowned, she immediately had my attention. "Yes, ma'am," I recalled all too vividly, "why do you ask?"

"That morning the Lord woke me early saying, 'Pray for Jimmy Swaggart.' I've followed your ministry for years and I immediately went to prayer until I felt that whatever danger there was had passed."

Briefly I explained the situation to the elderly woman. God had used her to thwart the plans of the enemy to snuff out my life. Her blue eyes seemed to twinkle as I thanked her profusely. "God be with you," she smiled and walked away. I never saw her again. In fact I don't even know her name. But I will never forget what her prayers did for me.

14
"THANK GOD, I'M BROKE!"

At thirty-four years of age, I became the youngest preacher ever to preach at the General Council of the Assemblies of God. Monday night was probably the toughest night to preach at the General Council. The people had been there almost a week and they had heard most of the well-known preachers in the denomination. Presidents of colleges and pastors of large churches had been the speakers before me.

I felt unworthy to preach to such a gathering of

the denomination's elite. But that night in Dallas the Holy Spirit moved before me, taking complete control.

Taking the story from the fifth chapter of Mark about the woman who had an issue of blood twelve years "and had suffered many things of many physicians, and had spent all that she had, and was nothing bettered, but rather grew worse . . ." I preached on the subject, "There Is a Remedy."

Many times I had experienced the anointing of the Holy Spirit on my preaching but never before as that night. Words, expressions, and thoughts all blended together as I exhorted the story of the woman who had faith enough to declare "if I may touch but his clothes, I shall be made whole."

Not once, but several times, the crowd of ten thousand came to its feet shouting and praising God. At times I thought the situation was going to get out of control. Hundreds of people in the balcony were singing, dancing and praising the Lord until I thought someone might accidentally dance over the retaining wall and fall to the floor below. The presence of God swept the entire coliseum from floor to ceiling.

Hundreds of people later told me it was the greatest service they had ever attended. One man expressed a fear that the compliments might cause me to share God's glory. But that would not happen now, not after all the years of struggle, disappointment, fear and frustration. After all the times of rejection, even being refused ordination, it would not happen. After some of my early attempts at preaching brought derision and ridicule I could not be so deceived. I knew it was all God—and none of me.

The next morning on the way back to Baton Rouge I cried every foot of the way. But it was for joy. "God," I sobbed softly, "I don't know if you consider that you owed me anything for these years of ministry . . . you don't. But if you thought you did, I was repaid a hundred times over last night."

A new sense of God's presence flooded me as I spoke. "Son," He seemed to answer, "this is simply my way of showing you that I've called you to this ministry. My hand is upon you. My approval is with you."

The radio ministry began to grow during the late summer of 1969. We added ten more stations. The realization that it required about $500 a day just to keep the program on the air was staggering. My mind began dwelling on the cost of the program. Gradually that $500 got bigger and bigger in my thoughts. As it did, my faith in God's ability to provide got smaller and smaller.

For several weeks I slept very little. Negative thoughts continually assaulted my mind. "You're going broke," the thoughts suggested. "Don't you know you can't raise $500 a day?"

I couldn't sleep. I couldn't eat. Once again my nerves were jangled. Slowly my health began to decline. It was almost a repeat of my battle with nerves years before.

At times I would look at Frances, sleeping peacefully in bed while I paced the floor, and I wanted to scream "Get up and worry!" But I didn't. She was always the picture of calm in the middle of a storm.

One night I found myself sitting on the edge of my bed holding my head in my hands. Voices had been speaking to me all night long, "You're going broke, you're going broke."

This night there was a new voice speaking, however. It was calm and reassuring. "What are you doing?" the Father asked.

"What do you mean what am I doing?" I retorted, "I'm going broke."

The Lord gently posed a question. "How much money do you have?"

"Money?" I mused. "I don't have any."

"Well then, how can you go broke?"

Those words were a ray of sunshine breaking through a gloomy day. I repeated them to myself: "How can you go broke?" I couldn't go broke, I was already broke. For the first time in weeks, I could see the lie Satan had been hurling at me. I was so excited about God's words to me I could hardly contain myself from shouting, "Thank God, I'm broke!"

As the radio program's audience grew, so did the mail response. This brought new problems. More equipment had to be purchased. Since I was already operating out of our house, the equipment ended up in the bedrooms, the kitchen and the living room, in addition to the garage which I had converted into an office.

Frances finally put her foot down. "Either build an office or move everything outside." She was right. I desperately needed an office.

In 1970, I was back at Detroit's Brightmoor Tabernacle with Pastor Bond Bowman for a nine-week revival. One night an elderly woman approached me after the service. Her name was Hallie Scott, affectionately called Mom.

"Brother Swaggart," she announced, "I want to give you two books."

The two books, one a study in faith and another on prayer, were by Kenneth Hagin, a widely respected Bible teacher and preacher. I stayed up most of the night reading. It was easy to grasp this truth because I had stumbled around the edges of it for years. I read the books through, crying most of the time. I read them both again and again. Through Kenneth Hagin I ran headlong into the truth of positive confession.

199

Obviously my prayer life had been a hit-or-miss proposition, now I had the Bible pattern for asking God for whatever I needed, and receiving it. It was a simple three-point plan.

First, I needed to find out if what I was seeking from God was His will. I could do this by checking His word. There were some things I would have to ask Him about since they were not mentioned in the Bible. But if it was there, I automatically knew.

Second, I didn't need to continue to repeat the request after first asking. That showed a lack of faith. All I needed was to begin thanking Him for the answer.

Third, I should not allow hindrances from the devil to block the answer. I needed to continue to confess what the Word said. That way my faith was put into action.

I returned to my Bible and read Mark 11:23. "Whosoever shall say unto this mountain, Be thou removed, and be thou cast into the sea; and shall not doubt in his heart, but shall believe that those things which he saith shall come to pass; he shall have whatsoever he saith."

Jesus used the words *say* or *saith* three times in that one single Scripture. What I said had a direct effect on my faith. It would wreck it or build it.

Now I had a formula and I was determined to

200

put it to work immediately. Years before Nannie had told me to believe God for big things. She had the right words but in reality, I didn't know how. Brother Hagin's teaching showed me the missing ingredient.

In that same Detroit meeting, I began to ask God for things in prayer. The answers began coming. I had suffered excruciating pain in my chest for many years. Doctors had been unable to determine the source, but when I asked God for healing, it came within two weeks.

Next, I began praying for that office building. As I asked the Lord for a piece of property for the ministry, I knew the request had been granted. I didn't have the money to buy any property. I didn't know where it was coming from, but I knew the property was ours. We needed it for God's work and that was it. I was going to conduct myself as if we already had the money for the property.

After getting back to Baton Rouge, I began to move in faith by calling a real estate office to set up an appointment. The next day an agent showed me some vacant lots on Goya Street, three blocks from Florida Boulevard, a main thoroughfare in Baton Rouge. The location was perfect.

Standing in the middle of the two lots, I asked the price. When the agent answered, I recognized the price was too high. I mumbled a reply and walked back to the car.

The agent came over to me. "Preacher, this is where you need to be," he suggested, patting me on the arm.

Once again I heard the voice of the Lord. "He has more faith than you."

I asked the price again. The man scratched his nose repeating the same figure. This time, I made a counteroffer of a lower figure.

"Fine," the agent agreed, "but I'll have to call you tomorrow after getting an answer from the owner. He might not accept your lower offer."

"Where am I going to get that money?" I asked myself after I got home. I didn't even have the lower figure of my counteroffer. The next morning the load was heavier than ever. Yet Frances was cheerful and encouraging about the property.

The real estate agent called later. "Reverend Swaggart," he announced, "I've got good news for you. The owner has accepted your offer. He will take it."

I stood listening to the agent talking, but not really hearing what he said. "The man will have to take it because I sure don't have it," I muttered to myself.

Two weeks later, still worrying where the money was going to come from, I was in Houston holding services at Lyndale Assembly of God with Pastor James McKeehan. One night during the service I mentioned something about needing money for the property.

Pastor McKeehan felt moved to give the congregation an opportunity to respond. While I was seated at the piano, Brother McKeehan walked over to me. "Here," he said, thrusting a check in my hand, "I want to give you this but don't say where it came from."

The check had been given by a man in the congregation. It was for several thousand dollars—enough to purchase the property.

There were more tears. I was overjoyed, yet ashamed. I had doubted God; yet, He had provided. Would I ever really learn to trust Him completely?

The opportunity to put my faith to work came immediately. The building would take four or five times as much money as the two lots had cost.

A design engineer drew up plans for the building and a building contractor gave me an estimate of $50,000. Frances and I began fervently praying over the matter.

While praying the Lord told me, "This is the man. He will build a good building. You should engage his services."

I called the contractor back and told him he had the job. "Reverend Swaggart," he asked, "do you have a loan for the building?"

I was dumbfounded for a few seconds. I hadn't even approached a bank about a loan. Money

203

from lending institutions was scarce, and loans were given only at high interest rates.

But there was faith in my heart. "God has told me to do it and I know it is the right thing to do," I thought to myself. "I don't know where the money is coming from. That is God's problem. It's not mine."

"Yes sir," I replied aloud, "arrangements have been made for the money."

Once again I faced a struggle. Voices of fear and doubt hounded me. "You are going to be made a laughingstock," the voices predicted. "You'll barely get the building started and have to stop. Everybody will know what you've done. Your ministry will be wrecked."

But I was learning. I knew God did not speak in doubt. He never talked about failure. Whenever these thoughts began to come to mind, I knew they were from the devil. Immediately I started rebuking the thoughts, refusing to dwell upon them and believing God for total victory.

As the building began taking shape, I knew the victory had been won. Each time the contractor presented a bill for payment, there was enough money in the checking account to pay it. I had moved into faith's wonderful land of provision.

By the summer of 1971, "The Camp Meeting

Hour" was widely accepted across the nation. But one morning the Lord awakened me about two o'clock. His presence was so real I lay in bed for thirty minutes, weeping. I thought my insides would burst. I knew God was trying to speak to me so I got out of bed and went to my prayer room.

There was no need to turn on a table lamp when I walked into the room. The room seemed already illuminated by the presence of God. I felt like Moses when the Lord told him he was standing on holy ground.

I didn't think I could bear it. I slumped to my knees, and then onto my face, sobbing.

"Son, I'm pleased with what you're doing," God said. "But you're going too slow with the radio effort. I will return before you get the job done. You must hurry. I want you to go on every radio station possible that will air a gospel program daily."

Was this really God? If I followed the direction of a wrong spirit, we would be ruined within a matter of days.

"Lord, when are you coming back?" I asked.

"Only I know the appointed time," He answered, "but I've told the Holy Spirit to hurry. You must hurry also." I felt at ease. A false spirit would have given me a date.

Immediately I began moving to do exactly what the Lord had instructed by placing the program on every station that would accept it. Ultimately I

205

retained an agency in Boston to handle the task. At first the agency was reluctant. They expressed a fear I was going too fast and too big. But the Lord continued to bless the ministry financially. The money was always supplied no matter the size of the bill.

As the radio audience grew, our record album sales also mushroomed. Sales were helped along, no doubt, by the fact two of my records were named number one gospel albums their respective years. "This Is Just What Heaven Means to Me" was number one in 1971, and "There Is a River" gained the same spot in 1972. At first Frances and I accepted the royalties from the records, but as the radio ministry grew the Lord told me He wanted all the money to go back into the ministry.

I didn't obey the Lord right away. The royalty money had been used to help build us a house and provide a few things for Donnie. But the Lord continued speaking to me. Each time I prayed, thoughts of the royalty money bore down upon me.

Several weeks later, Frances and I had gone up to the state capital to have a photograph taken for one of the album jackets. Afterwards I sat in the photographer's station wagon waiting for him to load equipment. "Now about these record albums," the Lord suddenly spoke to me.

"Father, would you take ninety percent and let me have ten percent?" I asked.

"You can have all of it," the Lord responded, "but you won't have my perfect will."

It was another step of commitment. But I knew it had to be done. As soon as I returned to the office, I contacted the ministry's attorney, Bill Treeby, advising him to draw up the necessary papers.

When I signed all of the royalties over to the ministry, a peace flooded my heart. I knew that I had been obedient to the Lord and it would ultimately bring blessing. Record sales tripled almost immediately, just in time to meet the increasing demands of "The Camp Meeting Hour" as it expanded into every major city in America.

The same morning the Lord directed me to expand the radio ministry, He also told me to make the Holy Spirit one of the focal points of the program. "Many people will be filled with the Holy Spirit," He had said, "and they will need teaching and instruction." He also warned me I would be opposed by religious people, that leaders who opposed the charismatic movement would view the program as a threat. Sure enough, they did.

I didn't realize it but many of the radio stations on which we broadcast were owned by evangelicals who vehemently opposed full gospel teaching—especially teaching which emphasized divine healing, miracles and speaking in tongues.

207

One of these stations, owned by a well-known evangelist, was one of our most responsive stations. Yet we were notified the program was being canceled.

"Why?" I asked.

"You can't preach your messages on our station," I was informed. "We don't agree with the way you teach the Holy Spirit, healing, miracles and speaking in tongues."

I tried to reason with the station's manager saying the evangelist who owned the station had always given the impression of being tolerant of other Christians with different views than his. The station manager agreed to see if a compromise could be worked out, but in spite of paying our bills on time and teaching with dignity, we were unceremoniously dumped from the station.

Hundreds of letters funneled into our office asking why the program was no longer on that particular station. There was nothing I could do. I couldn't get the program back on the air and I didn't feel free to announce over the air the real truth of the matter.

A number of other stations were also threatening to cancel. The situation looked desperate. I realized it was a direct attack of the devil. Nannie had furnished me with crucial training for times like this. I knew the answer was prayer, and plenty of it.

The only fight God had ever called me to wage

was the fight of faith. We moved forward in prayer and fasting, constantly confessing God's supremacy and binding the powers of darkness. Gradually the opposition receded. Only one other station canceled and I sensed we had won a great victory.

Demands for our meetings were growing at an incredible rate. I wanted to stay in Assembly of God churches, yet many people drove hundreds of miles and then couldn't get into the meetings because the buildings were too small. I finally set a rule that I wouldn't go into a church unless it seated at least a thousand people.

But soon, with the wide appeal of "The Camp Meeting Hour" and the records, even these auditoriums were not big enough. We advanced the figure to churches seating fifteen hundred people—and there just were not many Assembly of God churches that size.

One morning, standing on a church platform ready to preach, I sensed the Lord's presence had departed. I moved ahead, preaching the sermon. But there was no power. My words came back in my face. I followed through with the mechanical motions of an altar call, but it was all hollow—empty motions.

After the service mercifully ended, I sat down in

one of the platform chairs and bowed my head. "Lord, why?" I asked.

The Lord answered quickly. "Son, I've been trying to tell you for the last six months to leave the churches and go into the city auditoriums. You can stay here and die if you want, or you can do what I've told you."

"Lord," I replied, wiping my eyes, "I wouldn't go through this again for a million dollars. I'll obey you."

With the Lord's direction firmly entrenched in my heart, I moved out into weekend crusades, beginning first in Detroit.

With the help of pastors in the towns, we began developing a weekend crusade schedule that included almost every metropolitan area in America. All along the way the Lord confirmed His Word with signs following. He knew that thousands of denominational people, hungry for more of God, would come to a city auditorium more readily than to a Pentecostal church. And it was true, thousands came to the meetings. From Maine to California people were being saved, healed and filled with the Holy Spirit.

As always, teaching on the Holy Spirit was one of the things that attracted people. Many of them were openly seeking the Baptism. In the beginning all I knew was the old-time method of tarrying around some altar. But as hundreds came seeking to be filled, it was not humanly

210

possible to personally pray that many people through. Then the Lord showed me that with a few words of instruction and a simple prayer, hundreds could be filled with the Holy Spirit. In one Full Gospel Business Men's meeting in Toledo, I saw almost a thousand people filled with the Spirit following that method. This was surely a new day.

One of the first changes I made in our crusade meeting was with the music. I felt I was not giving people what they had come to hear. Many of them had heard the full orchestra sounds of my recordings, but in the meetings they only heard me playing and singing. Slowly the Lord began to assemble a good crusade band. Ray Ludwig, an organist, was hired followed by Dwain Johnson who played bass guitar and sang harmony with me. Then we added the Crawford brothers, Paul on the drums and Ron on the guitar.

Later we bought a new Peterbilt tractor with a forty-foot Great Dane trailer to transport all of our musical equipment, the albums, books and teaching tapes for the crusades. Gary Osborne quit a good-paying secular job to drive the rig to our meetings.

We used a large bus to haul the crusade team but discovered that mode of travel too costly —both in time and money. John Reuther joined us when we purchased a DC-3 airplane for crusade travel. Clearly in the 1970s, we had to adapt our methods to the changing times. But we never changed the message. That remained, as always, Jesus Christ the same yesterday, today, and forever (Hebrews 13:8).

15
A GOSPEL STATION FOR BATON ROUGE

Daddy called early one evening saying Pa Swaggart had suffered a crippling stroke. The doctors offered little hope for his survival. Years before Pa had been struck by a car paralyzing him from the waist down. I dropped everything and drove out to the nursing home north of Baton Rouge where Pa was being cared for.

As I walked into the place with its polished linoleum floors and hospital green walls, I reminisced about Pa. He had been more than just

213

a grandfather to me. He was more like a second father. I had stayed at his house as much as my own. Even when I was a child, he had talked to me like I was a grown man. Many of his personality traits had become mine.

Then it struck me: "We might lose him today." In spite of all the church services he had attended, in spite of Nannie's godliness, Pa might miss it. It was a terrible realization. Was it possible that Pa might miss heaven? Whatever I did, I had to make sure he was going to make it.

"Is he conscious?" I asked the white-frocked doctor caring for Pa.

"No, he's not," the doctor answered with a grim expression on his face.

"Would it hurt to pull the oxygen tent back," I inquired, "and let me try to talk with him?"

"I don't think so," he replied, "but I doubt seriously if he'll understand anything you say."

As the doctor and a nurse adjusted the oxygen tent, I wandered over to the room's double window to peer outside. I was deeply concerned about his salvation. I whispered a prayer. "Lord," I whispered, watching the afternoon shadows stretch across the nursing home lawn, "I love this old man. Heaven won't be the same if he's not there. I don't know if he's conscious or not, but if he isn't, would you let him regain his mental capacities long enough for me to talk with him?"

214

Pa's snow white hair framed his wrinkled face against the green hospital pillow like a halo. "Pa, this is Jimmy," I said taking his cold hand in mine. "I don't know if you can understand me but I've asked the Lord that you might."

He was motionless, but I continued talking. "This is it. The doctors have said you won't make it through the night. Nannie has already gone. So has mama and a lot of others. One day I will follow along. When I get there, you're going to be one of the first ones I look for, but I'm not sure all is well. I want to know."

Tears seeped out of his closed eyes and ran down his cheeks. Very gently he squeezed my hand. Peace flooded my heart. I knew he was telling me everything was all right. He had made things right with God.

I laid his hand down, wiped the tears from his face and slipped out of the room quietly as the nurse replaced the oxygen tent. Later that night, Pa joined Nannie and mama.

In 1973, I began production of our weekly television program. Actually I had been just as opposed to going into television as I had been radio. I guess fear played a large part in my reluctance. There were so many excellent

Christian television programs already being produced and I didn't feel as if I had anything special to offer. Yet the Lord continued prodding me until I obeyed.

At first we attempted to tape the program in Baton Rouge. The production was atrocious. Then we switched to New Orleans without any improvement. I kept telling Frances, "I can't do it, I can't do it."

Then one Sunday night I had a free evening in Baton Rouge and Frances and I decided to go to church. Riding along in the car, the Lord suddenly spoke to me. "The next time you say you can't do something I've told you to do, I'm going to count it as a sin. It will be like cursing me, and you'll have to ask me to forgive you." I looked out the window. The Lord didn't have to tell me He was talking about television—I knew it.

Something about the way God spoke to me melted my rebellion. From that day on, when I stepped before the camera, things happened. The Lord began immediately to bless our efforts.

The next month I stopped over in Nashville and walked into the studio where the nationally syndicated show, "Hee Haw," was produced. I was impressed with the facilities and found the production staff willing to help us. In prayer I turned the matter over to the Lord.

Utilizing the Nashville studio, the television

program took on a new flavor. I wanted to devote much of the program to good country-gospel music, so I hired some of the best I could find. Henry Slaughter, Jim Dumas and Joe Edwards joined us to improve our performance. With Phil Johnson of Heartwarming Records and a group of singers doing background vocals, the musical part of the program became top-drawer.

The format was simple, yet effective. The first fifteen or twenty minutes of the show was music, another ten minutes was used for a Bible message and the rest of the time was given to various announcements of our meetings and album offers.

The toughest part of taping the programs became the schedule. To coordinate my schedule with the studio's, we had to tape twenty-four of the half-hour programs in a single week's time. Humanly speaking, that seemed impossible. The only way it could ever be done was with the Lord's help.

Each time we taped the shows, the Lord's presence and anointing was so strong people in other areas of the sound stage would stop their work and listen. Some would cry. Since the program was geared to unsaved people, many times I stopped right in the middle of the program and offered people in the viewing audience an opportunity to accept Christ.

Hundreds of letters began pouring into the

office demonstrating what impact the program was having on people's lives. A man in Dallas wrote saying his father never darkened the doorway of a church but the old man religiously watched the program every Sunday with tears in his eyes. "I believe dad will be waiting for me in heaven," wrote the son, "because of your telecast."

The program crossed racial and ethnic barriers. One night I stepped off the platform of an auditorium in Norfolk, Virginia. I was tired and worn from the three-hour service. My clothes were damp with perspiration and I longed to get back to the hotel to rest.

As I moved toward the stage exit, a thick, muscular arm reached out and grabbed me. I turned and looked square into the rough face of a large black man.

"Brother Swaggart, I want to tell you something," the man said.

I stood listening. In fact, I had no choice.

"Just a few months ago, I was a Black Panther," he said softly. "My life was wrapped up in hate. It was my whole existence. After a night of drinking and partying, I flipped on the television one Sunday morning and your telecast came on. I started to turn it off but there was something about your music that stopped me.

"I got back in bed and the music began to sober me up like I was being delivered from some evil spirit. When the program was over, I knelt beside

218

the bed and gave my heart to Jesus. I've been filled
with the Holy Spirit and I'm now preaching the
gospel."

I thought back to the drawing power of God's
music. It drew my parents into a little Pentecostal
church in Louisiana, and it drew a Black Panther
to Jesus. Surely our God is a singing God, who
loves to hear his people join in on the chorus.

With "The Camp Meeting Hour" having such a
large audience, I thought it would be great if
Baton Rouge could have a Christian radio station.
I approached several stations looking into the
possibility of a purchase. The asking price
always seemed too high. But the desire to have a
station in Baton Rouge was obviously given me by
God. I knew better than to say "I can't." Instead I
began to search the mind of the Holy Spirit for a
solution.

During 1973, Tommy Waldron, who owned
two Christian radio stations in West Virginia,
called one night. "Did you know WLUX in Baton
Rouge is about to be put off the air by the FCC?"
he asked.

"No, I didn't," I answered. "Do you think
there's any chance somebody else could get the
license?"

"There might be," Tommy suggested. "Why don't you look into it?"

"I might just do that," I replied. "I've tried to convince radio stations here that gospel music could capture its share of the listening audience. But nobody would give it a chance. Maybe this is my chance to get Jesus on the air full-time."

Tommy gave me the name of a lawyer in Washington, D.C. who specialized in communications law. I contacted him. He immediately went to work filing the necessary papers to buy the station which was then in the hands of a court-appointed referee.

By law, the court had to allow anyone to bid on the station who had ever shown any interest in purchasing it. Along with myself, another man—tall, boisterous and constantly cursing—showed up. He was planning to make WLUX the number one rock music station in Baton Rouge.

That morning, the Lord spoke to me about the hearing. "Go to the bank," he directed. "Get all the money you can lay your hands on." I had no idea what the Lord had in mind but later that morning I went to the bank and withdrew $100,000 in negotiable securities. I put the securities in a bank bag and tucked them into an inside coat pocket. I felt a little foolish driving to the courthouse with all that money.

My heart sank as I listened to the radio

executive's claims about what he was going to do with the station. He was talking about all the big conglomerates behind him. "We plan to sink $250,000 into this station," he boasted.

"There's no way in the world I can get this station," I thought to myself. Then, I caught myself. That was saying "I can't." I reversed the process and began praising God for the station He was going to give me.

The court-appointed referee rapped on his gavel. "I am now opening the bidding on radio station WLUX as ordered by the FCC because of the status of the station being in bankruptcy court," the referee announced mechanically. "I represent the court."

The referee said the purchase price of the station would be $80,000. My lawyer bid $80,000 for the station, and the other man's lawyer entered the same bid.

"What do we do now?" asked one of the attorneys.

My lawyer spoke up. "In a case like this where there is a tie," he stated, "the law in the state of Louisiana says you must flip a coin. Whoever calls the winning side gets the bid."

I recognized I had a fifty-fifty chance of losing. Figuring I had little to lose I spoke up. "You're an arm of the court," I said to the referee, "and you're responsible for what little the station's creditors get."

"That's right," agreed the referee.

"This man has told us he has millions but how do you know he has a dime?" I asserted. "Talk is cheap."

I noticed the radio executive squirming in his seat. He tugged at his shirt collar. Sweat appeared on his forehead. "But what if he can't produce a dime," I continued. "You're an arm of the court and if you lose this money you'll be in hot water."

"That's right," the referee acknowledged. Looking at the other man he asked, "Do you have $80,000?"

"No . . . not with me," the man answered nervously, "but I can get it."

I spoke up again. "How do you know he can get it? What happens to the court and all the creditors if he can't?"

My lawyer had been punching me to keep quiet, but now he picked up on the situation. "Can you show me a financial statement saying you can get $80,000?" he questioned.

"No," he answered huffily, "but I can have it here Monday."

"But what if he can't," I interjected.

"Well, do you have $80,000?" he snapped looking at me. "Yeah, that's right," the man's attorney agreed, "you've been doing all this talking, do you have $80,000?"

My lawyer looked at me as if to say, "Why didn't you keep your mouth shut? At least we had a

222

fifty-fifty chance of winning. Now we don't have any."

But I knew I had more than enough money to win the bid. Reaching into my pocket, I located the bank bag and dropped it on the table. My lawyer's eyes looked like two fried eggs. Not a soul moved. Nobody said a word. They just stared at the money.

"Count it," I demanded, "I can put up mine. Can he put up his?"

The lawyers pulled the securities out. "There's $102,000 here," the referee announced. "I've never seen that much money in one stack in my life."

"It's negotiable," I pointed out, "just like cash dollars. I can prove my purchase money and you'd better accept it unless the other guy can put up his."

"Can you match this?" the referee asked.

"No," the man answered bluntly, "I can't. Obviously I'm in the wrong business. I ought to be a preacher." He grabbed his briefcase and stalked out of the room.

"In all of my years practicing law, I've never been in a hearing like this," my Washington lawyer remarked as we headed for the door.

Unfortunately that was only the first hurdle in getting the station. Although the referee had awarded me the bid for the station, the FCC turned down my ownership of WLUX. The commission said the station had been involved in numerous violations and it would close down the operations within six months.

My lawyer filed with the Court of Appeals to overturn the FCC's decision. In the meantime, the court-appointed referee appointed me as the manager of the station. I didn't tell him I knew nothing about operating the station. With the Lord's help we entered into a full-time format of gospel music and gospel related programs.

My lawyer suggested I collect all of the political muscle I could to help my position. I did that, too. It seemed useless. I was told the FCC ruling would probably be upheld on appeal.

For almost six months, the situation continued to look bleak. One day I was praying over the matter. "Lord," I said, "if it be your will, I want the station. But if it's not your will, I'll abide by it."

The Holy Spirit exploded within me. "Why are you praying that way?" He demanded. "Don't you think it's God's will for this station to broadcast the gospel?"

"I know that," I admitted.

"If you keep repeating 'if it be your will,' you're going to lose it," He stated firmly. "You are wrecking your faith."

I got back on my knees and asked God to forgive me. I had been praying a double-minded prayer. I knew those prayers didn't get any further than the ceiling of the room they were prayed in.

Before the six months was over, the Court of Appeals had overturned the FCC ruling against me. The station was ours. Prevailing prayer—the kind that Jesus said men ought always to do—had won out again.

Increased public visibility brought other problems to our ministry, however. With our radio and television programs constantly expanding into new areas of the country, our volume of mail increased so rapidly until we were handling more mail than anybody in the state of Louisiana.

The mail is our lifeblood. Donations and album orders came that way. In turn I was counseling people with problems. But as the volume of our mail soared, more people wrote saying they weren't receiving our records or tapes which we had mailed. We failed to get letters and billing statements from various companies. I finally woke up to the fact somebody was stealing our mail. The situation was rapidly creating a loss of revenue and credibility.

I called the postmaster but he didn't realize the size and scope of our problem. He thought we were talking about a few letters. Finally I got several members of the staff together and went down to his office. "We're actually losing thousands of pieces of mail," I informed him.

He was aghast. "I had no idea your operation was this big," he admitted. "We'll move immediately to get this problem halted."

Things looked bad. Our revenue had been cut in half. Our financial situation was becoming desperate, but the situation didn't worry me.

In a service one night I tried to explain my feelings to the Lord. "I don't want you to think I'm not concerned about this situation," I said, "but I've become so accustomed to teaching faith and believing your word, it's difficult for me to act any other way."

"You're acting exactly the way I want you to act," the Lord responded. "You're acting what you preach, and that's essential."

Eventually the post office discovered the mail was not being stolen at the main post office, but at a suburban branch. The man involved was soon arrested. Out on bail for the mail theft charge, he got involved in a brawl and killed a man. Ultimately he was tried for murder and sentenced to a long prison term.

For weeks afterward, rolls of our mail were located in ditches all over Baton Rouge where they had been tossed. For the next six months, I made every effort to replace all the orders our people had lost in our mail situation. God honored our efforts and before long we were back in business minus the problems. But it was a stern warning that the deeper we went with God, the more severe the attacks of Satan would be.

16
$35,000 A DAY
TO OPERATE

Crusade meetings, radio broadcasts, television programs, recording sessions combined to rush our lives at a hectic pace. The years seemed to speed past. No sooner had we moved into our new house with Donnie finally enrolling in a permanent school, than it was time for him to graduate. He was the first Swaggart in memory who ever graduated from high school.

After a year at Louisiana State University in Baton Rouge, Donnie transferred to

Southwestern Bible College, the same school Jerry Lee had attended years before.

With Donnie away at school, Frances and I felt an additional burden to pray for him. Our prayers were answered in a marvelous way in 1974 when Donnie married Debbie Robertson in a small Assembly of God church outside of Louisville, Mississippi. Later he left school and joined me in the ministry as director of our crusades. The first year he arranged all of our weekend crusades, which numbered thirty-five a year, handled all the auditorium arrangements and worked with the cooperating pastors in the towns. Debbie became a valuable office worker and a talented pianist with our crusade team.

Frances and I began to learn the importance of frequent vacations and good physical exercise, but still the ministry produced a tremendous pressure on body and mind. Preaching to thousands every weekend, the daily radio program, and the television—every phase of the work brought incredible pressures. There was the ever-present voice of the enemy. "You're going too far," he suggested frequently. "You're going to get into trouble with all of these projects. You'll go broke, bankrupt like many other preachers."

It was true. The ministry had expanded to astronomical proportions. I was busy in my office one day when dad walked into the room. He had been wandering through some new additions to our buildings on Goya Street, looking over the changes. The buildings were now the size of two football fields.

Still active in the ministry himself, dad had changed little over the years. He was still lean and carried himself erect on his six-foot-two-inch frame. His dark hair was now salted with gray, but he looked ten years younger than his sixty years.

"I can't get over it," he said smiling. "I just can't get over it."

"What's that?" I asked looking up from my stack of papers.

"Well," he answered taking a chair in front of me, "as I was walking through the offices the real extent of the ministry suddenly struck me."

I grinned, "And the greatest miracle is God chose a high school dropout like me to run it."

"The Camp Meeting Hour" was being aired on 550 stations—the largest daily gospel radio program in the world.

The telecast was on two hundred television stations with an additional two thousand television cable outlets. Over a million record albums were sold each year. An additional million cassette tapes were sent out each year. Thousands of pieces of mail arrived at our office daily, and over a million pieces of mail were sent from our offices each month. Our budget was now $35,000 a day. Not only did this stagger dad's imagination, it staggered mine.

231

We employed over one hundred and fifty people in our Baton Rouge office. The ministry also owned and operated five gospel radio stations in Dallas-Fort Worth, Oklahoma City, Pensacola, Baton Rouge and Bowling Green, Ohio.

When I was young I wanted to be rich. Fortunately the Lord took the desire away from me, for I had seen, first hand, how fame and money had ruined many Pentecostal preachers.

Once I was having lunch with Gordon Lindsay, founder of Christ for the Nations Institute in Dallas. His *Voice of Healing* magazine chronicled the exploits of many preachers during the healing revivals of the late 1940s and 1950s. He had seen many of them rise and fall.

That day I ticked off a list of men who had fallen by the wayside. "Brother Lindsay," I probed, "what happened to these men? They were mightily used of God."

He studied me carefully before answering. "Jimmy, there are not many men who can stand blessing. They can't stand the prosperity. They can't stand the fame. It goes to their heads. They start to think they are God. They think they can do it. Somehow they believe they're really special . . . and that's when they begin to decline."

"I know you're right," I agreed. "It's kinda like C.M. Ward says. They begin to believe their own advertising."

All of these thoughts were running through

my mind when Frances and I had dinner that night in a Dallas restaurant. I had to make a phone call before the dinner arrived and a strange thing happened while I was standing in a hallway of the fashionable restaurant dialing the number.

A man walked up to me. His eyes were bleary and his suit filthy. It had been days since he last shaved. "You're Jimmy Swaggart," he suggested.

"Yes, I am," I answered.

He just stood, tears filling his eyes. I first thought he was some poor soul who had messed himself up with alcohol. Then he told me his name. I almost dropped the telephone.

At one time he had been used of God in an outstanding national ministry. I had never met the man but was familiar with newspaper and magazine accounts of his miracle services. I didn't know what to say.

He did not say another word. He just looked deep into my eyes as if to say, "I blew it. I've made a fool out of myself. I've thrown it all away." Finally he turned and walked away. I was so shaken I hung up the telephone. I couldn't even eat when I got back to the table. I knew what had happened to that man could happen to anybody—even to me.

I knew that if the devil couldn't sideline me with immorality, money or fame, he would lead me into preaching some false doctrine which would make my ministry ineffective. The only defense was to stay grounded on the Bible, remain constant in prayer, and stay honest in all my affairs.

Once, just before a meeting in Norfolk, Virginia, I was praying when the Lord spoke to me. "I want you to give me an account for the money," He said.

His words stunned me. I wasn't even thinking about money. I had my mind on the services.

Carefully I thought over the situation. "Lord, I've spent the money on radio and television," I answered. "I've spent it on buildings and equipment. I believe I can stand before you and say I've handled it like you wanted me to do."

"Not only will you answer to me for how you spend the money," the Lord continued, "but in the judgment you will also answer to the people who have given."

A short time later I was in Detroit conducting a crusade. After closing the service, an elderly woman wearing an old, worn coat walked up. Her shoes were rundown at the heels and her appearance gave the impression of a hard life.

"Brother Swaggart, God said to give you this," she announced handing me a roll of bills. "It's for the radio."

I had never stopped anyone from making a donation, but something about this woman touched me. "Lady, how much money is this?" I asked.

"Thirty-two dollars."

"What kind of work do you do?" I inquired.

She stared at me briefly and dropped her head. "I scrub floors," she mumbled.

"You mean on your hands and knees?"

"Yes."

"How much money did you make last week?"

"Thirty-two dollars."

"You've given it all?"

"Every bit of it."

I was overwhelmed by her sacrifice, and I tried to give the money back.

"I won't take it back," she retorted. "You can leave it on the floor, but I won't take it back. God said to give it and I'm giving it."

I tried explaining God had other ways of getting His money. "You don't really have to give everything you have," I suggested. I could see she desperately needed clothes, maybe even food. Yet she refused.

When I finally turned and walked away from her, I was weeping. God was right. It was His money and I would have to give Him an accounting in the judgment. But I was also responsible to those whom God used to give. It's the most awesome responsibility in the world.

In 1976 we expanded the radio and television programs overseas. Now "The Camp Meeting Hour" is heard on powerful radio stations located in many strategic spots on the globe: Africa, India, Ireland, Hong Kong, the Philippines, Formosa, the West Indies and Central America. The Commission is clear—"be witnesses unto me to the uttermost parts of the earth."

As for me, I am determined to sing the same Jesus that I preach.

17
THE SPIRIT
LEADS ON

Jerry Lee recently visited with me in Fort Worth where I was speaking in a special church service one night. Along with him and his entourage came his son, Jerry Lee Lewis, Jr. A husky, good-looking boy, "Junior" was a talented musician with his dad's backup band. Although he was the same age as Donnie, they were not well acquainted. I had a deep affection for him.

The church was crowded that night as I preached on "New Life—what Jesus can do for you." The scene was repeated from many years before, as Jerry Lee came under conviction and wept most of the time he was in the service.

Junior had been in church infrequently. He had many problems. And he came forward that night sobbing. When others were leaving the altar, Junior came up and put his arms around me. He was a big boy who hadn't quite finished growing.

"Uncle Jimmy," he said with tears still glistening in his eyes, "I enjoyed this so much tonight."

"Junior, do you feel like the Lord came into your heart?" I asked.

"Oh, I know He did," he said. "I know He did." He looked around the church at the people. "I would give anything in the world if I could go with you," he said.

"You can if you want to," I answered, "that'll be fine with me."

He never really responded to what I said. We talked for a while and then he turned and walked away. As he did, my heart ached. I thought, "that could be my son going there—except for the grace of God."

I turned my thoughts to God and whispered a prayer for Junior. "Father, that boy can't live for you in the atmosphere he's in. I don't know what will have to be done. But if you have to take him home to heaven to insure his salvation—please do it."

I thought no more about it. Eight months later I was in Waxahachie, Texas, preaching at Southwestern Bible College when someone called saying Junior had been killed in a traffic accident. His jeep had overturned on a curve. Junior had died instantly of a broken neck.

I've never believed that God kills people. But there are situations that we sometimes don't understand. We can't see it all. In some cases I believe the Father calls people home. Junior was one of those.

Days later someone sent me a clipping from the *Detroit Free Press*. It contained a story about Jerry Lee. His problems always seemed to have been played out before a nationwide audience. I found his remarks prophetic that day.

The reporter recalled in the interview that Jerry Lee, along with Elvis Presley and several others who had been the originators of rock-and-roll music, were also the inspiration for the Beatles. "Did you ever have any idea what you helped start would affect so many lives for literally generations?" the reporter asked.

"There is no question it has had an effect," Jerry Lee answered. "There are millions on dope today who were influenced by the music. There are countless others who've gone off on every possible emotional trip. But had I known then, what I know now, I would have never played my first note on a piano."

Jerry Lee's career started out with glitter and glamour, fame and popularity. Many people follow that route. But the end of that road is disaster and confusion. It has been a story repeated many times by many people. "There is a way," Proverbs says, "which seemeth right unto a man, but the end thereof are the ways of death " (Proverbs 14:12).

I left the newspaper clipping on my desk and wandered out of my office and into our main business room. People were scurrying everywhere, typewriters clattering, phones ringing. We had started out so small, Frances and I. Jerry Lee was at his zenith—making millions and playing to thousands, while I was back in the swamps preaching to stumps. But now, twenty years down the road, God had sustained us and His Word had prevailed.

I knew I had to continue praying for him. I had made a commitment to never stop as long as there was breath. Just like that promise I made to see mama, I made a promise for Jerry Lee. I will not be satisfied until I know he has entered the Kingdom of God.

Henry Culbreth, who had played such an important role in my life when he pastored in

Ferriday during the early 1940s, was in our services in Phoenix during a recent crusade. He had just returned from a long missionary stay in Indonesia, and was now teaching at an Indian school in Arizona.

I told the audience the role Brother Culbreth played during the formative years of my life and asked him to come forward for a word of personal testimony. What he said stunned me.

"Back many years ago," he recalled, "Jimmy Swaggart attended a morning prayer meeting with about twelve other people in Ferriday. There was a prophecy given during the meeting that God was going to use somebody in that room in a worldwide ministry. The person would have a great influence on many lives coming to Christ."

"I didn't believe the prophecy when I first heard it," Brother Culbreth explained honestly. "I looked at that little group and I knew the older folks were too advanced in age to fulfill the prophecy. I looked at the kids—Jimmy, Mickey, David and a few others—and I just knew there was no way those kids could be used like that."

Tears were in Brother Culbreth's eyes as he motioned me back to the microphone. He put his arm around me. "But in the last few years, as I have seen Jimmy Swaggart's ministry develop and attain worldwide stature," he said, "I know that prophecy was from God. It has indeed been fulfilled."

241

The meetings at Norfolk's Scope had been superb. There were large crowds and a tremendous response. Many were saved and filled with the Holy Spirit.

After the meeting all fourteen members of the traveling crusade team were on board the DC-3 bound for Baton Rouge. Our pilot John Reuther told me it was going to be a blustery night. Sure enough, we ran straight into a solid line of thunderstorms. I later learned that thirty-seven people were killed in air crashes that night.

As we proceeded across the darkened Carolina skies, the rain fell in such torrents I couldn't even see the wing tips. Knowing I could do nothing but put my fate in God's hands, I lay back to rest from the exhausting three day crusade.

The ride suddenly became bumpy. The plane seemed to rise five hundred feet in the air and then drop another five hundred feet. I heard the left engine quit. It sputtered, then quit again. That happened four times before the engine roared back to life.

I knew we had problems. It was night, the rain was heavy and we were flying over mountains. John decided to land at Asheville, North Carolina, rather than continue on. With the help of the radar operator and the Asheville tower, we finally reached the ground safely.

Asheville Airport lies between two rugged mountain peaks. But with God's help we came down out of the black skies to a perfect landing. As we deplaned and headed for the terminal building, my thoughts wandered back to Ferriday and growing up. My mind traced over various spots—preaching to the stumps, holding a revival at my home church, the offer to record for Sun Records, the struggles, the problems, and above all, the victories.

I turned and looked back at the DC-3. Floodlights cast an eerie glow over the plane against a backdrop of rain, fog and a bleak, dark night. I recalled a poem I heard A. N. Trotter quote many times:

I can see far down the mountain
Where I've wandered many years
Often hindered on my journey
By the ghosts of doubts and fears.

Broken vows and disappointments
Thickly strewn along the way
But the Spirit has led unerring
To the land I hold today.

Somehow it seemed my entire life was contained in that poem. All forty-one years of it. That week our crusade team had been in Norfolk, Virginia. The next week we would be in Kansas City, followed by Dayton, St. Louis, and Canton. In December we would fill an entire week with television taping before leaving for Israel. A new recording session was being planned. The list appeared endless as the work of the Lord went on.

In my own strength I could never make it. But

There is a river that flows from deep within,
There is a fountain that frees the soul from sin.
Come to the water,
There is a vast supply,
There is a river that never shall run dry.

Write for a free, semi-monthly newsletter, *The Evangelist,* to:
      Jimmy Swaggart
      Baton Rouge, Louisiana 70821